FAST
pasta

THE AUSTRALIAN Women's Weekly

FAST
pasta

contents

The simple things in life are often the best. This adage is a perfect way to describe one of the most popular meals in the world – pasta. The universal love for pasta is due in part to its versatility, variety of shapes and sizes, and also in the selection of vegetables, herbs, cheeses, meats and seafood you can add to make it a meal bursting with flavour. Marrying pasta with a complementary sauce is an ideal solution to creating a fast meal. All you need is a pot of boiling water, a handful of pasta and a few basic ingredients to create something special for children and adults alike. Pasta is a low GI food and contains less than 0.5g of fat per ½ cup serving – making it a good choice for diabetics, athletes and the health conscious. This selection of recipes takes next to no time to prepare and includes rich, velvety sauces, hearty meat and seafood sauces and simple tomato-based sauces, all of which are sure to impress even the most discerning pasta lover. You'll also find tips on how to cook the perfect al dente pasta and a pasta identification guide. Pasta has never been so much fun, nor so fast; buon appetito!

To cook pasta

Overcooked pasta can ruin even the most delicious sauce.

Dried pasta

Gradually add pasta to a large saucepan of boiling water, making sure water does not go off the boil. When cooking 'long' pastas, such as spaghetti, hold strands at one end until the submerged end becomes soft in the water. Gradually lower strands, coiling them neatly. Cook pasta until just tender; it should be 'al dente' (to the tooth) – tender but firm.

Cooking times for pasta will vary according to individual manufacturers so check pasta regularly to ensure it does not overcook.

Pasta should only be rinsed after draining if being used in a cold dish, or not being served immediately. In these cases, rinse pasta under cold running water to stop the cooking process, then drain.

Uncooked dried pasta can be stored up to a year in a cool, dry place. Cooked pasta can be refrigerated, covered, for 3 days.

Fresh pasta

Fresh pasta is cooked in much the same way as dried pasta, however, it requires much less cooking time.

Gradually add fresh pasta to a large saucepan of boiling water, making sure water does not go off the boil. Allow to cook for a few minutes until pasta is 'al dente'. It will not take long, so check pasta regularly to ensure it does not overcook.

Why is pasta so good?

Pasta is usually made from wheat flour or semolina and water. It is a great source of carbohydrates and is fortified with folic acid, which may protect against certain cancers and heart disease. The complex carbohydrates give slow-release energy, making it popular amongst athletes and also good for diabetics. There is less than 0.5g of fat in a ½-cup serving of pasta, so it is perfect for those watching their weight.

Pasta shapes

It is important to choose a pasta shape to complement your sauce. Generally, long, thin pastas suit light, thin sauces; thicker pastas suit heavier sauces; smaller shapes with ridges or holes are perfect for chunkier sauces; and small pastas, such as risoni and macaroni, are good in soups.

  We have specified a pasta for each recipe, however, if you prefer, simply substitute any pasta of your choice.

Know your pasta

With literally hundreds of types available, these are most familiar.

elbow macaroni
(small)

cellentani

tortellini

penne

bow ties (farfalle)

tortiglioni

orecchiette

rigatoni

macaroni

pappardelle

garganelli

spiral (fusilli)

tagliatelle

elbow macaroni
(large)

shells

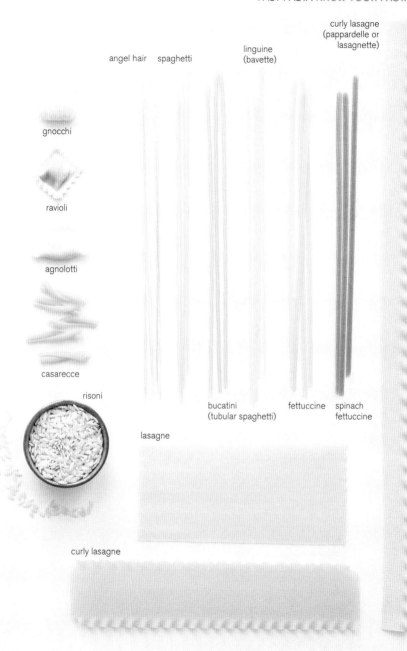

curly lasagne
(pappardelle or
lasagnette)

linguine
(bavette)

angel hair   spaghetti

gnocchi

ravioli

agnolotti

casarecce

risoni

bucatini
(tubular spaghetti)   fettuccine   spinach
fettuccine

lasagne

curly lasagne

11

salads

Mediterranean pasta salad

Originally a homemade specialty from the Italian region of Puglia, orecchiette translates as "little ears", a shape this short pasta actually resembles. You can use any small pasta you like if you cannot find orecchiette.

250g orecchiette pasta
2 tablespoons drained sun-dried tomatoes, chopped coarsely
1 small red onion (100g), sliced thinly
1 small green capsicum (150g), sliced thinly
½ cup coarsely chopped fresh flat-leaf parsley
sun-dried tomato dressing
1 tablespoon sun-dried tomato pesto
1 tablespoon white wine vinegar
2 tablespoons olive oil

1 Cook pasta in large saucepan of boiling water, uncovered, until just tender; drain. Rinse under cold water; drain.
2 Meanwhile, make sun-dried tomato dressing.
3 Place pasta in large bowl with remaining ingredients and dressing; toss gently to combine.
sun-dried tomato dressing place ingredients in screw-top jar; shake well.

on the table in 25 minutes
serves 4 **per serving** 12.0g total fat (1.9g saturated fat); 1400kJ (335 cal); 46.0g carbohydrate; 8.8g protein; 3.7g fibre

Artichoke pasta salad

375g elbow macaroni
350g artichoke hearts in oil
400g semi-dried tomatoes
¼ cup loosely packed fresh oregano leaves
400g bocconcini cheese, chopped coarsely
¼ cup (60ml) sherry vinegar
2 cloves garlic, crushed

1 Cook pasta in large saucepan of boiling water, uncovered, until just tender; drain. Rinse under cold water; drain.
2 Meanwhile, drain artichokes over small bowl; reserve 2 tablespoons of the oil. Discard any remaining oil; quarter artichokes.
3 Place pasta and artichoke in large bowl with tomatoes, oregano, cheese and combined vinegar, garlic and reserved oil; toss gently to combine.

on the table in 25 minutes
serves 4 **per serving** 21.1g total fat (10.8g saturated fat); 3340kJ (799 cal); 100.3g carbohydrate; 40.7g protein; 20.5g fibre
tip packed in a leak-proof container, this salad is perfect for a picnic.

Greek penne salad

250g penne pasta
250g fetta cheese
4 medium tomatoes (760g), seeded, sliced thinly
1 lebanese cucumber (130g), seeded, sliced thinly
1 small red onion (100g), sliced thinly
¾ cup (120g) kalamata olives, seeded
¾ cup (120g) large green olives, seeded
dressing
⅓ cup (80ml) olive oil
⅓ cup (80ml) white vinegar
1 teaspoon white sugar
2 tablespoons finely chopped fresh flat-leaf parsley

1 Cook pasta in large saucepan of boiling water, uncovered, until just tender; drain. Rinse under cold water; drain.
2 Meanwhile, make dressing.
3 Cut cheese into baton-shape pieces about the same size as the pasta.
4 Place pasta and cheese in large bowl with tomato, cucumber, onion, olives and dressing; toss gently to combine.
dressing place ingredients in screw-top jar; shake well.

on the table in 30 minutes
serves 4 **per serving** 34.2g total fat (12.4g saturated fat); 2667kJ (638 cal); 60.6g carbohydrate; 19.8g protein; 4.4g fibre

Warm salami and tomato pasta salad

375g orecchiette pasta
200g thinly sliced hot salami
1/3 cup (60g) toasted pine nuts, chopped
250g cherry tomatoes
250g grape tomatoes, halved
1/3 cup fresh flat-leaf parsley leaves
1/3 cup torn fresh basil leaves
1/4 cup (20g) shaved pecorino cheese
dressing
1/3 cup (80ml) olive oil
1/4 cup (60ml) red wine vinegar
2 cloves garlic, crushed

1 Cook pasta in large saucepan of boiling water, uncovered, until just tender; drain. Rinse under cold water; drain.
2 Meanwhile, cook salami in large frying pan, stirring, until crisp; drain on absorbent paper.
3 Make dressing.
4 Place pasta, dressing, salami, pine nuts, tomatoes, herbs and cheese in large bowl; toss gently to combine.
dressing place ingredients in screw-top jar; shake well.

on the table in 25 minutes
serves 4 **per serving** 50.1g total fat (10.4 saturated fat); 3494kJ (836 cal); 68.2g carbohydrate; 25.6g protein; 6.4g fibre

Greek lamb and pasta salad

600g lamb fillets
1 tablespoon olive oil
1 tablespoon finely chopped fresh oregano
500g tortiglioni pasta
1 medium red onion (170g), cut into thin wedges
500g cherry tomatoes, halved
2 lebanese cucumbers (260g), chopped coarsely
1 large green capsicum (350g), chopped coarsely
1⅔ cups (200g) seeded kalamata olives
200g fetta cheese, crumbled
lemon and oregano dressing
½ cup (125ml) olive oil
½ cup (125ml) lemon juice
1 tablespoon finely chopped fresh oregano

1 Combine lamb, oil and about a third of the oregano in large bowl. Cook lamb, in batches, in oiled frying pan until browned and cooked as desired. Cover lamb; stand 5 minutes, slice thinly.
2 Meanwhile, cook pasta in large saucepan of boiling water, uncovered, until just tender; drain. Rinse under cold water; drain.
3 Make lemon and oregano dressing.
4 Place lamb and pasta in large bowl with onion, tomato, cucumber, capsicum, olives and dressing; toss gently to combine. Top with cheese; sprinkle with remaining oregano.
lemon and oregano dressing place ingredients in screw-top jar; shake well.

on the table in 30 minutes
serves 6 **per serving** 40.1g total fat (12.4g saturated fat); 3357kJ (803 cal); 71.7g carbohydrate; 38.3g protein; 7.3g fibre

Bacon and corn pasta salad with mustard dressing

500g large pasta crests
1 tablespoon olive oil
250g button mushrooms, halved
4 rashers rindless bacon (250g), chopped coarsely
230g baby corn
1 medium red onion (170g), chopped coarsely
1 large avocado (320g), chopped coarsely
1 cup fresh flat-leaf parsley leaves
mustard dressing
1 cup (250ml) bottled caesar salad dressing
1 tablespoon wholegrain mustard

1 Cook pasta in large saucepan of boiling water, uncovered, until just tender; drain. Rinse under cold water; drain.
2 Meanwhile, heat oil in large frying pan, add mushroom and bacon and cook stirring, until beginning to brown. Remove mixture from pan then add corn and cook, stirring, until browned all over.
3 Make mustard dressing.
4 Place pasta, mushroom mixture and corn in large bowl with onion, avocado, parsley and dressing; toss gently to combine.
mustard dressing combine ingredients in small bowl or jug.

on the table in 30 minutes
serves 6 **per serving** 39.4g total fat (6.0g saturated fat); 2943kJ (704 cal); 65.2g carbohydrate; 19.2g protein; 7.0g fibre

Warm gnocchi salad

200g jar char-grilled capsicums in oil
2 tablespoons red wine vinegar
2 cloves garlic, crushed
⅓ cup (80ml) olive oil
500g potato gnocchi
½ cup (80g) black olives
340g jar marinated artichoke hearts, drained, quartered
1 medium red onion (150g), sliced thinly
½ cup firmly packed fresh basil leaves
⅓ cup (40g) toasted walnuts

1 Drain capsicums, reserve oil – you will need ¼ cup (60ml) oil. Slice capsicums thinly.
2 Combine reserved capsicum oil with vinegar, garlic and olive oil in a screw-top jar; shake well.
3 Cook gnocchi in large saucepan of boiling water, simmer, uncovered, about 3 minutes or until gnocchi float; drain.
4 Combine capsicum, olives, artichokes, onion, basil and hot gnocchi in large bowl. Add oil mixture. Sprinkle with walnuts.

on the table in 15 minutes
serves 4 **per serving** 27.7g total fat (3.8g saturated fat); 2011kJ (481 cal); 45.6g carbohydrate; 9.3g protein; 6.8g fibre

Pasta and chicken salad

Penne is an Italian word for the old-fashioned quill pen, a tool which this ridged macaroni, cut into short lengths on the diagonal, resembles. You can use any small pasta you like instead of penne.

600g chicken breast fillets
250g penne pasta
1 large red capsicum (350g), chopped coarsely
4 large egg tomatoes (360g), seeded, chopped coarsely
6 green onions, sliced thinly
200g fetta cheese, chopped coarsely
80g baby rocket leaves
dressing
¼ cup (60ml) olive oil
⅓ cup (80ml) red wine vinegar
1 teaspoon dijon mustard
1 teaspoon white sugar

1 Place chicken in medium saucepan, cover with boiling water; return to a boil. Reduce heat, simmer, uncovered, about 10 minutes or until chicken is cooked through. Cool chicken, still in poaching liquid, 5 minutes. Remove chicken from pan, slice thickly; discard poaching liquid.
2 Cook pasta in large saucepan of boiling water, uncovered, until just tender; drain. Rinse under cold water; drain.
3 Meanwhile, make dressing.
4 Place chicken and pasta in large bowl with remaining ingredients and dressing; toss gently to combine.
dressing place ingredients in screw-top jar; shake well.

on the table in 35 minutes
serves 4 **per serving** 29.8g total fat (10.6g saturated fat); 2842kJ (680 cal); 48.6g carbohydrate; 52.2g protein; 4.0g fibre

Chilli tuna pasta salad

300g large pasta shells
250g fresh green beans, trimmed, halved
2 x 185g cans tuna in chilli oil
⅓ cup coarsely chopped fresh flat-leaf parsley
⅓ cup firmly packed fresh basil leaves, torn
2 tablespoons drained baby capers
150g baby rocket leaves
¼ cup (60ml) olive oil
¼ cup (60ml) lemon juice
2 cloves garlic, crushed
2 teaspoons white sugar

1 Cook pasta in large saucepan of boiling water, uncovered, until just tender; drain. Rinse under cold water; drain.
2 Meanwhile, boil, steam or microwave beans until just tender; drain. Rinse under cold water; drain.
3 Drain tuna; reserve oil. Place tuna in large bowl; flake with fork. Add pasta and beans with herbs, capers and rocket; toss gently to combine.
4 Place remaining ingredients and reserved oil in screw-top jar; shake well. Drizzle over salad; toss gently to combine.

on the table in 30 minutes
serves 6 **per serving** 16.8g total fat (2.5g saturated fat); 1626kJ (389 cal); 37.9g carbohydrate; 19.6g protein; 3.6g fibre

Chicken and asparagus pasta salad

You will need to purchase a large barbecued chicken weighing about 900g for this recipe.

500g macaroni
250g asparagus, trimmed, chopped coarsely
3 cups (480g) shredded cooked chicken
200g button mushrooms, sliced
⅓ cup chopped fresh chives
dressing
⅓ cup (80g) light sour cream
½ cup (150g) mayonnaise
1 tablespoon lemon juice
1 tablespoon wholegrain mustard

1 Cook pasta in large saucepan of boiling water, uncovered, until just tender; drain. Rinse under cold water; drain.
2 Meanwhile, boil, steam or microwave asparagus until just tender; drain.
3 Make dressing.
4 Place pasta and asparagus in large bowl with dressing and remaining ingredients; toss gently to combine.
dressing combine ingredients in small bowl or jug.

on the table in 25 minutes
serves 4 **per serving** 26.7g total fat (6.9g saturated fat); 3453kJ (826 cal); 94.5g carbohydrate; 47.5g protein; 6.5g fibre
tip this salad should be assembled just before serving.

Fresh salmon and pasta salad

You will need about 600g fresh peas for this recipe.

500g bow tie pasta
1½ cups (240g) shelled fresh peas
500g salmon fillets
⅔ cup (160g) sour cream
1 tablespoon lemon juice
2 teaspoons water
2 tablespoons green peppercorns, rinsed, drained
1 tablespoon coarsely chopped fresh dill
2 trimmed celery stalks (200g), sliced thinly on the diagonal
⅓ cup coarsely chopped fresh chives

1 Cook pasta in large saucepan of boiling water, uncovered, adding peas
about halfway through cooking time; drain when pasta is just tender.
2 Meanwhile, cook salmon, uncovered, in large heated oiled frying pan
until cooked as desired. Drain on absorbent paper.
3 Combine sour cream, juice, the water, peppercorns and dill in small bowl.
4 Place salmon in large bowl; using fork, flake salmon. Add celery, chives,
sour cream mixture, pasta and peas; toss gently to combine.

on the table in 30 minutes
serves 6 **per serving** 17.6g total fat (8.5g saturated fat); 2236kJ
(535 cal); 62.0g carbohydrate; 28.7g protein; 5.5g fibre
tip frozen peas can be thawed and substituted for fresh peas; add them
to the pasta just before draining it.

Hot-smoked salmon salad

While most of the smoked salmon we buy has been cold-smoked (cured at a low temperature for a fairly long time), hot-smoked salmon (cured at high temperatures for just a few hours) is generally moister and not as salty; it doesn't, however, have the same keeping properties as cold-smoked.

375g fettuccine
400g hot-smoked salmon
100g mizuna
1 medium avocado (250g), chopped coarsely
1 lebanese cucumber (130g), halved, sliced thinly
1 small fennel bulb (200g), trimmed, sliced thinly
¼ cup (50g) drained baby capers, rinsed
dressing
1 tablespoon dijon mustard
2 teaspoons white sugar
2 tablespoons olive oil
1 tablespoon lemon juice

1 Cook pasta in large saucepan of boiling water, uncovered, until just tender; drain. Rinse under cold water; drain.
2 Meanwhile, remove any skin and bones from salmon; flake salmon into large pieces. Combine salmon in large bowl with mizuna, avocado, cucumber, fennel and capers.
3 Make dressing.
4 Add pasta and dressing to salmon mixture; toss gently to combine.
dressing place ingredients in screw-top jar; shake well.

on the table in 30 minutes
serves 4 **per serving** 24.9g total fat (4.5g saturated fat); 2742kJ (656 cal); 69.4g carbohydrate; 35.3g protein; 5.8g fibre

Pasta salad with garlic vinaigrette

Purple basil, also known as opal basil, has an intense aroma and longer shelf-life than sweet basil.

375g penne pasta
200g sun-dried tomatoes in oil
½ cup (80g) toasted pine nuts, chopped coarsely
400g bocconcini cheese, chopped coarsely
1 small red onion (100g), sliced thinly
12 fresh purple basil leaves, torn
12 fresh basil leaves, torn
2 cloves garlic, crushed
1 tablespoon dijon mustard
¼ cup (60ml) lemon juice

1 Cook pasta in large saucepan of boiling water, uncovered, until just tender; drain. Rinse under cold water; drain.
2 Meanwhile, drain tomatoes; reserve oil. Slice tomatoes thickly.
3 Place pasta and tomato in large bowl with nuts, cheese, onion and both basils.
4 Combine reserved sun-dried tomato oil and remaining ingredients in screw-top jar; shake well. Drizzle over salad; toss gently to combine.

on the table in 25 minutes
serves 6 **per serving** 21.8g total fat (7.6g saturated fat); 2245kJ (537 cal); 56.4g carbohydrate; 24.4g protein; 8.2g fibre
tips this recipe should be assembled just before serving. You can use any short pasta you like instead of the penne.

Macaroni tuna salad

250g small macaroni
200g green beans, halved
200g yellow string beans, halved
415g can tuna in oil, drained, flaked
1 small red onion (80g), sliced thinly
¼ cup finely chopped fresh flat-leaf parsley
dressing
½ cup (125ml) olive oil
¼ cup (60ml) lemon juice
2 cloves garlic, crushed
2 teaspoons curry powder

1 Cook pasta in large saucepan of boiling water, uncovered, until just tender; drain. Rinse under cold water; drain.
2 Meanwhile, boil, steam or microwave beans until just tender; drain. Rinse under cold water; drain.
3 Make dressing.
4 Place pasta and beans in large bowl with dressing and remaining ingredients; toss gently to combine.
dressing place ingredients in screw-top jar; shake well.

on the table in 30 minutes
serves 4 **per serving** 40.9g total fat (6.0g saturated fat); 2863kJ (685 cal); 46.7g carbohydrate; 30.3g protein; 5.5g fibre
tip yellow string beans are sometimes called butter beans; you can substitute them with chopped snake beans if desired.

Chicken pasta salad with roasted capsicum, fetta and walnut

You will need to purchase a large barbecued chicken weighing about 900g for this recipe.

300g frilled pasta shells
270g jar char-grilled capsicum in oil
150g fetta cheese, chopped coarsely
3 cups (480g) shredded cooked chicken
1/3 cup (35g) toasted walnuts, chopped coarsely
1 cup loosely packed fresh basil leaves
1/4 cup (60ml) red wine vinegar
1 clove garlic, crushed
2 teaspoons wholegrain mustard

1 Cook pasta in large saucepan of boiling water, uncovered, until just tender; drain. Rinse under cold water; drain.
2 Meanwhile, drain capsicum, reserving 1/3 cup of the oil; chop capsicum coarsely. Place capsicum and pasta in large bowl with cheese, chicken, walnuts and basil.
3 Combine reserved oil with remaining ingredients in a screw-top jar; shake well. Drizzle over chicken mixture; toss gently to combine.

on the table in 15 minutes
serves 4 **per serving** 26.2g total fat (9.2g saturated fat); 2713kJ (649 cal); 53.8g carbohydrate; 46.8g protein; 4.1g fibre
tips goat cheese or any soft, crumbly cheese can be used instead of the fetta. Toasted pecan halves make a nice change from walnuts.

Hot rigatoni salad with cauliflower

Rigatoni, ridged hollow tubes of pasta that look like a short, fat version of penne, are a perfect shape to capture and hold the sauce in this recipe. You will need a piece of broccoli weighing about 600g and a piece of cauliflower weighing about 500g for this recipe.

375g rigatoni pasta
⅓ cup (80ml) olive oil
5 cloves garlic, chopped coarsely
1½ cups (105g) stale breadcrumbs
350g cauliflower florets
350g broccoli florets
⅓ cup (80ml) lemon juice
1 cup coarsely chopped fresh flat-leaf parsley
½ cup (40g) toasted flaked almonds

1 Cook pasta in large saucepan of boiling water, uncovered, until just tender; drain. Rinse under cold water; drain.
2 Meanwhile, heat 2 tablespoons of the oil in large frying pan; cook garlic and breadcrumbs, stirring, until browned lightly. Place in large serving bowl.
3 Heat remaining oil in same pan; cook cauliflower and broccoli, in batches, stirring, until almost tender. Add vegetables to bowl with pasta, juice, parsley and nuts; toss to combine.

on the table in 35 minutes
serves 4 **per serving** 26.3g total fat (3.3g saturated fat); 2909kJ (696 cal); 85.7g carbohydrate; 22.9g protein; 11.7g fibre

Spinach and prosciutto salad

375g large spiral pasta
12 thin slices prosciutto (240g)
150g baby spinach leaves
2 tablespoons wholegrain mustard
2 cloves garlic, crushed
½ cup (125ml) olive oil
¼ cup (60ml) lemon juice

1 Cook pasta in large saucepan of boiling water, uncovered, until just tender; drain. Rinse under cold water; drain.
2 Meanwhile, cook prosciutto, in batches, in large heated frying pan until browned and crisp; drain on absorbent paper, chop coarsely.
3 Place pasta and prosciutto in large bowl with spinach and combined remaining ingredients; toss gently to combine.

on the table in 20 minutes
serves 4 **per serving** 33.3g total fat (5.5g saturated fat); 2763kJ (661 cal); 65.3g carbohydrate; 22.8g protein; 4.6g fibre

Pasta caesar salad

200g large pasta shells
2 rashers rindless bacon (130g), chopped finely
1 medium cos lettuce, torn
2 hard-boiled eggs, chopped coarsely
2 small avocados (400g), chopped coarsely
½ cup (40g) shaved parmesan cheese
caesar dressing
1 egg
2 cloves garlic, quartered
2 tablespoons lemon juice
1 teaspoon dijon mustard
8 anchovy fillets, drained
¾ cup (180ml) olive oil

1 Cook pasta in large saucepan of boiling water, uncovered, until just tender; drain. Rinse under cold water; drain.
2 Meanwhile, cook bacon in small frying pan, stirring, until browned and crisp; drain on absorbent paper.
3 Make caesar dressing.
4 Place pasta and bacon in large bowl with lettuce, hard-boiled egg and avocado; pour over half of the dressing, toss gently to combine.
5 Divide salad among serving plates; drizzle with remaining dressing, sprinkle with cheese.
caesar dressing blend or process egg, garlic, juice, mustard and anchovies until smooth; with motor operating, gradually add oil, processing until dressing thickens.

on the table in 30 minutes
serves 4 **per serving** 66.1g total fat (13.1g saturated fat); 3469kJ (830 cal); 36.0g carbohydrate; 22.6g protein; 4.0g fibre

Sweet chilli prawn salad

250g rigatoni pasta
1kg cooked large prawns, shelled, tails intact
2 green onions, chopped finely
1 tablespoon coarsely chopped fresh watercress
1 tablespoon coarsely chopped fresh coriander
1 lebanese cucumber (130g), chopped coarsely
½ cup (125ml) sweet chilli sauce
1 teaspoon sesame oil
1 tablespoon lime juice

1 Cook pasta in large saucepan of boiling water, uncovered, until just tender; drain. Rinse under cold water; drain.
2 Place pasta in large bowl with prawns, onion, watercress, coriander, cucumber and combined remaining ingredients; toss gently to combine.

on the table in 20 minutes
serves 4 **per serving** 2.3g total fat (0.4g saturated fat); 1530kJ (366 cal); 49.7g carbohydrate; 33.2g protein; 4.0g fibre
tip we used thai sweet chilli sauce; if you use a less sweet, more concentrated chilli sauce, we suggest you use far less, tasting as you go.

Seafood salad

1 teaspoon olive oil
1 small brown onion (80g), sliced thinly
1 clove garlic, crushed
500g seafood marinara mix
375g large pasta shells
1 tablespoon dry white wine
½ cup (150g) mayonnaise
1 teaspoon lemon juice
2 teaspoons worcestershire sauce
⅓ cup (80ml) tomato sauce
¼ teaspoon tabasco sauce
1 tablespoon chopped fresh flat-leaf parsley
100g baby rocket leaves

1 Heat oil in large frying pan; cook onion and garlic, stirring, until onion softens. Add marinara mix; cook, stirring, about 5 minutes or until seafood is cooked through. Place marinara mixture in large bowl, cover; refrigerate 10 minutes.
2 Meanwhile, cook pasta in large saucepan of boiling water, uncovered, until just tender; drain. Rinse under cold water; drain.
3 Place marinara mixture and pasta in large bowl with combined wine, mayonnaise, juice, sauces and parsley; toss gently to combine.
4 Serve seafood salad on rocket leaves.

on the table in 35 minutes
serves 4 **per serving** 16.4g total fat (2.4g saturated fat); 2696kJ (645 cal); 84.5g carbohydrate; 35.6g protein; 4.7g fibre

Salmon and pasta salad with dill dressing

375g small pasta shells
2 x 415g cans red salmon, drained
2 small fennel bulbs (400g), sliced thinly
1 large red onion (300g), chopped finely
350g cornichons, drained, halved
1 tablespoon finely chopped capers
dill dressing
⅓ cup finely chopped fresh dill
½ cup (125ml) white wine vinegar
½ cup (125ml) lemon juice
⅔ cup (160ml) olive oil
1 tablespoon wholegrain mustard

1 Cook pasta in large saucepan of boiling water, uncovered, until just tender; drain. Rinse under cold water; drain.
2 Meanwhile, remove any bones from drained salmon; flake salmon with a fork.
3 Make dill dressing.
4 Place pasta and salmon in large bowl with dressing and remaining ingredients; toss gently to combine.
dill dressing place ingredients in screw-top jar; shake well.

on the table in 15 minutes
serves 4 **per serving** 58.0g total fat (10.9g saturated fat); 4448kJ (1064 cal); 82.2g carbohydrate; 50.5g protein; 6.6g fibre

Tuna with shells, capers, olives and green beans

375g small pasta shells
200g green beans, halved
3 x 125g cans tuna slices in spring water, drained
150g seeded black olives, halved
1 medium red capsicum (200g), sliced thinly
dressing
¼ cup (60ml) olive oil
¼ cup (60ml) white wine vinegar
2 tablespoons drained capers, chopped coarsely
1 clove garlic, crushed

1 Cook pasta in large saucepan of boiling water, uncovered, until just tender; drain. Rinse under cold water; drain.
2 Meanwhile, boil, steam or microwave beans until just tender; rinse under cold water, drain.
3 Make dressing.
4 Place pasta and beans in large bowl with dressing and remaining ingredients; toss gently to combine.
dressing place ingredients in screw-top jar; shake well.

on the table in 30 minutes
serves 4 **per serving** 16.6g total fat (2.7g saturated fat); 2374kJ (568 cal); 75.9g carbohydrate; 25.2g protein; 5.6g fibre

Ravioli salad

You will need about 500g of fresh broccoli for this recipe. You can use any variety of ravioli you like so long as the filling does not include any meat.

375g spinach and ricotta ravioli
4 rashers rindless bacon (250g), chopped coarsely
250g (2 cups) broccoli florets
250g cherry tomatoes, halved
2 tablespoons finely shredded fresh basil
½ cup (125ml) olive oil
¼ cup (60ml) white wine vinegar
2 tablespoons sun-dried tomato pesto

1 Cook pasta in large saucepan of boiling water, uncovered, until just tender; drain. Rinse under cold water; drain.
2 Meanwhile, cook bacon in small frying pan, stirring, until browned and crisp; drain on absorbent paper.
3 Boil, steam or microwave broccoli until just tender, drain. Rinse under cold water; drain.
4 Place pasta, bacon and broccoli in large bowl with tomato, basil and combined remaining ingredients; toss gently to combine.

on the table in 30 minutes
serves 4 **per serving** 37.5g total fat (8.8g saturated fat); 2044kJ (489 cal); 17.2g carbohydrate; 19.0g protein; 5.7g fibre
tip you can use any kind of prepared pesto you like in the dressing: roasted vegetable is a good alternative.

Lemon tuna and pasta salad

375g bow tie pasta
¼ cup (60g) olive tapenade
1 teaspoon finely grated lemon rind
¾ cup (180ml) lemon juice
½ cup (125ml) olive oil
2 tablespoons white wine vinegar
1 tablespoon white sugar
1 teaspoon salt
425g can tuna in oil, drained, flaked
1 large green cucumber (400g), seeded, chopped finely
4 trimmed celery stalks (400g), sliced thinly
4 green onions, sliced thinly
2 fresh small red thai chillies, chopped finely
⅓ cup finely chopped fresh mint

1 Cook pasta in large saucepan of boiling water, uncovered, until just tender; drain. Rinse under cold water; drain.
2 Meanwhile, combine tapenade with rind, juice, oil, vinegar, sugar and salt in small bowl.
3 Place pasta and tapenade mixture in large bowl with remaining ingredients; toss gently to combine.

on the table in 35 minutes
serves 4 **per serving** 41.7g total fat (6.1g saturated fat); 3444kJ (824 cal); 75.9g carbohydrate; 33.1g protein; 6.3g fibre
tip tapenade, a paste of pureed olives, is available from supermarkets and delicatessens.

Pasta salad with chicken livers and pistachios

Curly lasagne, sometimes called pappardelle or lasagnette, is a long pasta, about midway in width between conventional lasagne and fettuccine. Cut into thin ribbons, it's the perfect size to toss with the livers and leaves in this salad.

250g curly lasagne
500g chicken livers, trimmed
150g wild rocket leaves
1 tablespoon finely grated lemon rind
⅓ cup (50g) toasted shelled pistachios
lemon mustard dressing
2 teaspoons dijon mustard
1 clove garlic, crushed
⅓ cup (80ml) olive oil
¼ cup (60ml) lemon juice

1 Cook pasta in large saucepan of boiling water, uncovered, until just tender; drain. Rinse under cold water; drain. Cut pasta strips lengthways into 2cm ribbons.
2 Meanwhile, halve each chicken liver; cook, in batches, in large heated oiled frying pan about 2 minutes or until browned and cooked as desired.
3 Make lemon mustard dressing.
4 Place pasta and liver in large bowl with dressing and remaining ingredients; toss gently to combine.
lemon mustard dressing place ingredients in screw-top jar; shake well.

on the table in 25 minutes
serves 4 **per serving** 30.0g total fat (4.9g saturated fat); 1956kJ (468 cal); 20.1g carbohydrate; 28.7g protein; 3.1g fibre

Asparagus and two-cheese pasta salad

For a different flavour, if you prefer, you can use 100g of goats or blue cheese instead of half of the ricotta.

500g bow tie pasta
500g asparagus, trimmed
100g parmesan cheese
½ cup (80g) toasted pine nuts
1 cup (200g) ricotta cheese, crumbled
4 green onions, sliced thinly
dijon dressing
⅓ cup (80ml) white wine vinegar
⅓ cup (80ml) olive oil
1 clove garlic, crushed
1 teaspoon dijon mustard

1 Cook pasta in large saucepan of boiling water, uncovered, until just tender; drain. Rinse under cold water; drain.
2 Meanwhile, cut asparagus to 8cm lengths. Boil, steam or microwave until tender.
3 Using a vegetable peeler, shave the parmesan into flakes.
4 Make dijon dressing.
5 Place pasta, asparagus and parmesan in large bowl with dressing and remaining ingredients; toss gently to combine.
dijon dressing place ingredients in screw-top jar; shake well.

on the table in 25 minutes
serves 6 **per serving** 31.6g total fat (8.3g saturated fat); 2592kJ (620 cal); 59.0g carbohydrate; 22.5g protein; 4.5g fibre

Deli pasta salad

You can use any short pasta you like instead of the spirals. The vegetables used in this recipe are available from most delicatessens, or bottled from supermarkets.

500g large spiral pasta
150g drained char-grilled eggplant, chopped
150g drained char-grilled capsicum, chopped
150g semi-dried tomatoes
150g sliced salami, cut into strips
⅓ cup small fresh basil leaves
pesto dressing
1 cup (250ml) bottled italian dressing
2 tablespoons basil pesto

1 Cook pasta in large saucepan of boiling water, uncovered, until just tender; drain. Rinse under cold water; drain.
2 Meanwhile, make pesto dressing.
3 Place pasta and dressing in large bowl with remaining ingredients; toss gently to combine.
pesto dressing place ingredients in screw-top jar; shake well.

on the table in 20 minutes
serves 6 **per serving** 29.1g total fat (5.9g saturated fat); 2658kJ (636 cal); 70.6g carbohydrate; 19.0g protein; 7.8g fibre

Sesame beef and pasta salad

500g spaghettini
1kg beef rump steak, sliced thinly
1 clove garlic, crushed
2 tablespoons sweet chilli sauce
1 tablespoon peanut oil
1 medium yellow capsicum (200g), sliced thinly
1 medium carrot (120g), sliced thickly
100g trimmed watercress
150g snow peas, trimmed, sliced thinly
2 teaspoons sesame seeds, toasted
sesame dressing
⅓ cup (80ml) peanut oil
½ teaspoon sesame oil
⅓ cup (80ml) rice vinegar
2 tablespoons light soy sauce
1 tablespoon lemon juice
1 green onion, sliced thinly

1 Cook pasta in large saucepan of boiling water, uncovered, until just tender; drain. Rinse under cold water; drain.
2 Meanwhile, combine beef, garlic and sauce in large bowl. Heat oil in wok; stir-fry beef mixture, in batches, until beef is browned all over and cooked as desired.
3 Make sesame dressing.
4 Place pasta, beef mixture and dressing in large bowl with vegetables; toss gently to combine. Sprinkle with sesame seeds.
sesame dressing place ingredients in screw-top jar; shake well.

on the table in 35 minutes
serves 6 **per serving** 22.1g total fat (5.0g saturated fat); 2776kJ (664 cal); 61.8g carbohydrate; 51.0g protein; 5.3g fibre

Warm tuna pasta salad

500g spiral pasta
2 x 425g cans tuna in oil
440g can corn kernels, drained
1 small red onion (100g), sliced thinly
1 medium red capsicum (200g), sliced thinly
2 trimmed celery stalks (200g), sliced thinly
¼ cup coarsely chopped fresh flat-leaf parsley
¼ cup (75g) mayonnaise
1 tablespoon yogurt
1 clove garlic, crushed
1 teaspoon finely grated lemon rind
2 tablespoons lemon juice
2 tablespoons wholegrain mustard

1 Cook pasta in large saucepan of boiling water, uncovered, until just
tender; drain. Rinse under cold water; drain.
2 Meanwhile, drain tuna; reserve 2 tablespoons of the oil.
3 Place pasta, tuna, corn, onion, capsicum, celery and parsley in large bowl.
4 Combine mayonnaise, yogurt, garlic, rind, juice, mustard and reserved
oil in small bowl or jug. Add to pasta mixture; toss gently to combine.

on the table in 30 minutes
serves 4 **per serving** 32.4g total fat (5.0g saturated fat); 4147kJ
(992 cal); 108.7g carbohydrate; 60.7g protein; 8.9g fibre

Greek chicken pasta salad

You will need to purchase a large barbecued chicken weighing about 900g for this recipe.

375g small shell pasta
¼ cup coarsely chopped fresh oregano
½ cup (125ml) olive oil
¼ cup (60ml) lemon juice
3 cups (480g) shredded cooked chicken
1 medium red onion (170g), sliced thinly
500g cherry tomatoes, quartered
2 lebanese cucumbers (260g), chopped coarsely
1 large green capsicum (350g), chopped coarsely
1 cup (120g) seeded kalamata olives
280g jar marinated artichoke hearts, drained, chopped coarsely
200g fetta cheese, chopped coarsely

1 Cook pasta in large saucepan of boiling water, uncovered, until just tender; drain. Rinse under cold water; drain.
2 Meanwhile, place 2 tablespoons of the oregano, oil and juice in a screw-top jar; shake well.
3 Place pasta in large bowl with chicken, onion, tomato, cucumber, capsicum, olives, artichoke, cheese and dressing; toss gently to combine.
4 Top salad with remaining oregano.

on the table in 30 minutes
serves 4 **per serving** 51.4g total fat (14.5g saturated fat); 4205kJ (1006 cal); 79.8g carbohydrate; 52.6g protein; 8.8g fibre
tip you can use the oil from the artichokes in the dressing if you wish.

cheese
+eggs

Fettuccine carbonara

4 rashers rindless bacon (250g), sliced thinly
⅓ cup (80ml) cream
pinch ground paprika
1 egg
1 egg yolk
¾ cup (60g) grated parmesan cheese
250g fettuccine
30g butter

1 Cook bacon in large frying pan over low heat until crisp. Add cream and paprika to pan; stir until combined.
2 Place egg, egg yolk and cheese in medium bowl; beat until combined.
3 Cook pasta in large saucepan of boiling water, uncovered, until just tender; drain.
4 Add pasta and butter to bacon mixture; toss over low heat until combined. Add egg mixture to pan; toss until combined.

on the table in 35 minutes
serves 4 **per serving** 25.1g total fat (14.6g saturated fat); 2082kJ (498 cal); 43.5g carbohydrate; 23.5g protein; 2.1g fibre
tip pancetta can be substituted for bacon in this recipe.

Baked three cheese pasta

375g macaroni
300ml cream
⅓ cup (80ml) vegetable stock
1¼ cups (150g) grated fontina cheese
⅓ cup (75g) crumbled gorgonzola cheese
1¼ cups (100g) coarsely grated parmesan
1 teaspoon dijon mustard
2 tablespoons finely chopped fresh flat-leaf parsley
1 tablespoon finely chopped fresh chives

1 Preheat oven to 200°C/180°C fan-forced.
2 Cook pasta in large saucepan of boiling water, uncovered, until just tender; drain.
3 Heat cream and stock in medium saucepan until hot. Remove pan from heat, add fontina, gorgonzola and half of the parmesan; stir until melted. Add mustard and herbs; season to taste with freshly ground black pepper. Combine cream mixture with pasta.
4 Pour cheesy pasta mixture into 2.5-litre (10-cup) ovenproof dish. Top with remaining parmesan. Bake, uncovered, 15 minutes or until browned.

on the table in 35 minutes
serves 4 **per serving** 59.2g total fat (38g saturated fat); 3917kJ (937 cal); 66.4g carbohydrate; 35.4g protein; 3.3g fibre

Fettuccine boscaiola

2 teaspoons olive oil
200g button mushrooms, sliced thickly
2 cloves garlic, crushed
200g shaved ham, chopped coarsely
¼ cup (60ml) dry white wine
1¼ cups (310ml) cream
500g fettuccine
2 tablespoons coarsely chopped fresh chives

1 Heat oil in large saucepan; cook mushroom, garlic and ham, stirring, until ingredients are browned lightly. Add wine, bring to a boil; boil, uncovered, until wine reduces by half.
2 Add cream to mushroom mixture; reduce heat, simmer, uncovered, until sauce thickens slightly.
3 Meanwhile, cook pasta in large saucepan of boiling water, uncovered, until just tender; drain.
4 Add pasta to sauce with half of the chives; toss gently to combine. Serve sprinkled with remaining chives.

on the table in 30 minutes
serves 4 **per serving** 39.2g total fat (23.4g saturated fat); 3478kJ (832 cal); 87.8g carbohydrate; 26.8g protein; 5.7g fibre

Gnocchi al quattro formaggi

Pasta with four cheeses is one of the most delectable (and among the richest!) of all the Italian classic sauces. Here we team it with gnocchi, but it also marries well with fettuccine or tagliatelle.

¼ cup (60ml) dry white wine
1 cup (250g) mascarpone cheese
1 cup (120g) coarsely grated fontina cheese
½ cup (40g) coarsely grated parmesan cheese
¼ cup (60ml) milk
625g gnocchi
75g gorgonzola cheese, crumbled

1 Add wine to large saucepan; boil, uncovered, until wine reduces by half. Reduce heat, add mascarpone; stir until mixture is smooth. Add fontina, parmesan and milk; cook, stirring, until cheeses melt and sauce is smooth.
2 Meanwhile, cook gnocchi in large saucepan of boiling water, uncovered, until gnocchi rise to the surface and are just tender; drain.
3 Add gnocchi to sauce with gorgonzola; toss gently to combine.
4 Serve sprinkled with freshly cracked black pepper.

on the table in 20 minutes
serves 4 **per serving** 56.8g total fat (36.7g saturated fat); 3436kJ (822 cal); 47.4g carbohydrate; 27.0g protein; 3.6g fibre

Bucatini with baked ricotta

375g bucatini pasta
2 x 270g jars marinated eggplant in oil
2 cloves garlic, crushed
2 x 400g cans tomatoes
½ teaspoon cracked black pepper
300g baked ricotta cheese, chopped coarsely

1 Cook pasta in large saucepan of boiling water, uncovered, until just tender; drain.
2 Meanwhile, cook undrained eggplant and garlic in large saucepan, stirring, until fragrant.
3 Add pasta to eggplant mixture with undrained crushed tomatoes and pepper; toss over medium heat until combined. Gently stir in cheese.

on the table in 20 minutes
serves 4 **per serving** 16.7g total fat (7.3g saturated fat); 2286kJ (547 cal); 73.6g carbohydrate; 21.1g protein; 7.9g fibre
tip baked ricotta is available from most supermarkets, delicatessens and specialty cheese shops. It is a baked fresh ricotta cheese; egg whites, paprika and oil are often added.

Ricotta, red capsicum and chilli pappardelle

¼ cup (60ml) olive oil
2 cloves garlic, crushed
½ teaspoon dried chilli flakes
4 large red capsicum (1.1kg), sliced thinly
¼ cup (60ml) water
375g pappardelle pasta
¼ cup finely chopped fresh chives
2 cups (400g) ricotta cheese
½ cup (100g) ricotta cheese, sliced, extra

1 Heat oil in large saucepan, add garlic and chilli; cook, stirring, until fragrant. Add capsicum and water; simmer, covered, 15 minutes or until capsicum is soft.
2 Meanwhile, cook pasta in large saucepan of boiling water, uncovered, until just tender; drain.
3 Add pasta and chives to capsicum mixture. Break ricotta into large pieces, add to pan; toss gently to combine.
4 Serve pasta topped with extra ricotta. Sprinkle with extra dried chilli and drizzle with a little extra olive oil, if desired.

on the table in 30 minutes
serves 4 **per serving** 29.3g total fat (11.1g saturated fat); 2867kJ (686 cal); 74.9g carbohydrate; 27.5g protein; 6.1g fibre
tip the capsicum mixture can be made several hours ahead; reheat capsicum mixture and complete recipe just before serving.

Rigatoni with brie, walnut and mushroom sauce

1 tablespoon olive oil
1 clove garlic, crushed
200g button mushrooms, halved
½ cup (125ml) dry white wine
2 tablespoons wholegrain mustard
600ml cream
375g rigatoni pasta
200g brie cheese, chopped coarsely
1 cup (100g) toasted walnuts, chopped coarsely
¼ cup coarsely chopped fresh chives

1 Heat oil in large frying pan; cook garlic and mushrooms, stirring, until mushrooms are just tender. Add wine; boil, uncovered, until wine reduces by half.
2 Add mustard and cream to mushroom mixture; cook, stirring, until sauce thickens slightly.
3 Meanwhile, cook pasta in large saucepan of boiling water, uncovered, until just tender; drain.
4 Return pasta to pan, add sauce and remaining ingredients; toss gently to combine.

on the table in 25 minutes
serves 4 **per serving** 102.6g total fat (54.1g saturated fat); 5601kJ (1340 cal); 69.7g carbohydrate; 28.9g protein; 6.4g fibre

Blue cheese penne and tomatoes

6 egg tomatoes (360g), halved
1 tablespoon olive oil
300g penne pasta
125g blue cheese, crumbled
125g tub light cream cheese, softened
1 cup (80g) finely grated parmesan cheese
200g baby spinach leaves

1 Preheat grill. Place tomatoes, cut-side up, on grill tray; drizzle with
oil. Place under grill about 10 minutes or until soft and lightly browned;
remove from grill, cover to keep warm.
2 Meanwhile, cook pasta in large saucepan of boiling water, uncovered,
until just tender. Drain and return to pan.
3 Immediately add blue cheese, cream cheese, half of the parmesan and
spinach to pasta; toss until well combined.
4 Place pasta mixture into shallow 2.5-litre (10-cup) ovenproof dish;
sprinkle with remaining parmesan. Place under grill until top is golden
brown. Serve with tomatoes.

on the table in 35 minutes
serves 4 **per serving** 27.4g total fat (14.8g saturated fat); 2433kJ
(582 cal); 54.2g carbohydrate; 27.1g protein; 4.9g fibre

Cheese and spinach tortellini with gorgonzola sauce

750g cheese and spinach tortellini
30g butter
2 tablespoons plain flour
1 cup (250ml) milk
¾ cup (180ml) cream
100g gorgonzola cheese, chopped coarsely
¼ cup loosely packed fresh flat-leaf parsley leaves

1 Cook pasta in large saucepan of boiling water, uncovered, until just tender; drain.
2 Meanwhile, melt butter in medium saucepan, add flour; cook, stirring, about 2 minutes or until mixture thickens and bubbles.
3 Gradually stir in milk and cream; bring to a boil. Reduce heat, simmer, uncovered, until sauce boils and thickens. Remove from heat; stir in cheese.
4 Combine pasta and sauce; sprinkle with parsley to serve.

on the table in 20 minutes
serves 4 **per serving** 49.3g total fat (31.8g saturated fat); 2876kJ (688 cal); 36.5g carbohydrate; 23.6g protein; 3.6g fibre
tips you can substitute the tortellini with ravioli or even gnocchi, if you like. Gorgonzola is a traditional northern Italian creamy blue cheese. The double-cream bavarian blue or blue castello can be substituted, but will lack that particular tempered piquancy of a ripe gorgonzola.

Spaghetti with herbed ricotta

500g spaghetti
2¼ cups (450g) ricotta cheese
3 egg yolks
¾ cup (180ml) milk
⅓ cup coarsely chopped fresh flat-leaf parsley
¼ cup coarsely chopped fresh basil
3 green onions, chopped finely
2 cloves garlic, crushed
¼ cup (20g) finely grated pepato cheese

1 Cook pasta in large saucepan of boiling water, uncovered, until just tender; drain.
2 Meanwhile, whisk ricotta, egg yolks and milk in large bowl until smooth; stir in herbs, onion, garlic and pepato.
3 Add pasta to ricotta mixture; toss gently to combine. Sprinkle with freshly cracked pepper to serve.

on the table in 25 minutes
serves 4 **per serving** 20.2g total fat (10.8g saturated fat); 2809kJ (672 cal); 89.4g carbohydrate; 30.0g protein; 4.9g fibre

Bacon and cheese macaroni

375g macaroni
500g broccoli, trimmed, chopped finely
1 tablespoon olive oil
1 medium brown onion (150g), chopped finely
4 rashers rindless bacon (250g), sliced thinly
2 cloves garlic, crushed
300ml cream
1 cup (80g) grated parmesan cheese
½ cup (60g) grated cheddar cheese

1 Cook pasta in large saucepan of boiling water, uncovered, until just tender. Add broccoli 1 minute before end of cooking time; drain. Return to pan, cover to keep warm.
2 Meanwhile, heat oil in large frying pan; cook onion, bacon and garlic, stirring, until bacon is crisp. Add cream, cook, stirring, until sauce thickens slightly, stir in half of the parmesan.
3 Preheat grill to high.
4 Add sauce to pasta, stir to combine. Spoon mixture into an oiled 2-litre (8-cup) ovenproof dish. Top with combined remaining parmesan and cheddar. Grill until cheese is browned lightly.

on the table in 25 minutes
serves 4 **per serving** 51.9g total fat (30.4g saturated fat); 3754kJ (898 cal); 68.9g carbohydrate; 35.8g protein; 7.3g fibre

Tagliatelle with mushrooms and peppercorn brie

400g tagliatelle pasta
200g peppercorn brie cheese, chilled
60g butter
6 green onions, chopped finely
2 cloves garlic, crushed
300g button mushrooms, sliced thinly
200g flat mushrooms, sliced thinly
½ cup (125ml) dry white wine
1 cup (250ml) vegetable stock
1 tablespoon wholegrain mustard
¼ cup (25g) drained sun-dried tomatoes, sliced thinly
1 cup (250ml) cream
2 teaspoons finely chopped fresh thyme

1 Cook pasta in large saucepan of boiling water, uncovered, until just tender; drain.
2 Meanwhile, remove rind from cheese; slice cheese thinly.
3 Heat butter in large saucepan; cook onion, garlic and mushrooms, stirring, until mushrooms are soft.
4 Add wine and stock; simmer, uncovered, until liquid reduces by half.
5 Add mustard, tomato, cheese, cream and thyme; stir until cheese melts.
6 Serve sauce on pasta with extra chopped fresh thyme, if desired.

on the table in 35 minutes
serves 4 **per serving** 56.0g total fat (35.6g saturated fat); 3967kJ (949 cal); 74.3g carbohydrate; 28.6g protein; 8.0g fibre

Angel hair frittata

100g angel hair pasta
1 tablespoon vegetable oil
1 small leek (200g), chopped coarsely
2 cloves garlic, crushed
¼ cup (20g) finely grated parmesan cheese
200g fetta cheese, crumbled
60g spinach leaves, chopped coarsely
½ cup (120g) sour cream
¼ teaspoon ground nutmeg
6 eggs, beaten lightly

1 Cook pasta in large saucepan of boiling water, uncovered, until just tender; drain.
2 Meanwhile, heat oil in 20cm frying pan; cook leek and garlic, stirring, until leek softens.
3 Combine pasta and leek mixture in large bowl with cheeses, spinach, sour cream, nutmeg and egg. Pour mixture into same frying pan; cook, covered, over low heat 10 minutes.
4 Preheat grill.
5 Remove cover from pan; grill about 5 minutes or until frittata sets and top browns lightly. Stand in pan 5 minutes before serving.

on the table in 30 minutes
serves 4 **per serving** 38.1g total fat (19.6g saturated fat); 2190kJ (524 cal); 19.7g carbohydrate; 25.3g protein; 2.4g fibre
tip angel hair pasta, the finest of pastas, produces the best results in this frittata because it lends a smooth-textured consistency.

Fettuccine alfredo

375g fettuccine
90g butter, chopped coarsely
⅔ cup (150ml) cream
1 cup (80g) finely grated parmesan cheese
2 tablespoons finely chopped fresh flat-leaf parsley

1 Cook pasta in large saucepan of boiling water, uncovered, until just tender; drain. Return pasta to pan to keep warm.
2 Meanwhile, place butter and cream in medium saucepan, stir over low heat until butter melts and combines well with cream; remove from heat. Add cheese; stir until sauce is blended and smooth.
3 Spoon sauce over hot pasta; toss well to combine. Serve sprinkled with parsley.

on the table in 20 minutes
serves 4 **per serving** 42.2g total fat (27.2g saturated fat); 3014kJ (721 cal); 65.2g carbohydrate; 19.0g protein; 3.2g fibre

Ricotta gnocchi in fresh tomato sauce

500g firm ricotta cheese
1 cup (80g) finely grated parmesan cheese
½ cup (75g) plain flour
2 eggs, beaten lightly
1 tablespoon olive oil
4 medium tomatoes (760g), chopped coarsely
6 green onions, sliced thinly
2 tablespoons coarsely chopped fresh oregano
2 tablespoons balsamic vinegar
2 tablespoons olive oil, extra
½ cup (40g) shaved parmesan cheese

1 Bring large saucepan of water to a boil.
2 Combine ricotta, grated parmesan, flour, egg and oil in large bowl. Drop rounded tablespoons of mixture into boiling water; cook, without stirring, until gnocchi float to the surface. Remove from pan with slotted spoon; drain. Cover to keep warm.
3 Combine tomato, onion, oregano and vinegar in medium bowl.
4 Divide warm gnocchi among serving bowls, top with fresh tomato sauce; drizzle with extra oil, sprinkle with shaved parmesan.

on the table in 30 minutes
serves 4 **per serving** 40.6g total fat (18g saturated fat); 2383kJ (570 cal); 19.4g carbohydrate; 32.1g protein; 3.3g fibre

Macaroni cheese

250g elbow macaroni
60g butter
⅓ cup (50g) plain flour
3 cups (750ml) milk
2 cups (250g) coarsely grated pizza cheese

1 Cook pasta in large saucepan of boiling water, uncovered, until just tender; drain.
2 Meanwhile, melt butter in medium saucepan, add flour; cook, stirring, about 2 minutes or until mixture thickens and bubbles. Gradually stir in milk; cook, stirring, until sauce boils and thickens.
3 Preheat grill to high.
4 Stir pasta and half of the cheese into sauce; pour mixture into shallow 2-litre (8-cup) baking dish. Sprinkle with remaining cheese; grill until cheese melts and is browned.

on the table in 25 minutes
serves 4 **per serving** 34.2g total fat (21.8g saturated fat); 2876kJ (688 cal); 60.9g carbohydrate; 32.8g protein; 2.5g fibre
tip unlike the traditional macaroni cheese, this quick version doesn't have to go into the oven – great for when you want dinner on the table fast.

Bow ties with asparagus and grilled haloumi

375g bow tie pasta
750g asparagus, trimmed, chopped coarsely
250g haloumi cheese, sliced thinly
1 medium avocado (250g), sliced thinly
2 tablespoons coarsely chopped fresh chives
1 tablespoon finely grated lemon rind
¼ cup (60ml) lemon juice
⅓ cup (80ml) olive oil
1 teaspoon white sugar

1 Cook pasta in large saucepan of boiling water, uncovered, until just tender; drain. Rinse under cold water; drain.
2 Meanwhile, boil, steam or microwave asparagus until just tender; drain.
3 Cook cheese, in batches, in medium oiled frying pan until browned lightly; drain on absorbent paper.
4 Place pasta, asparagus and cheese in large bowl with avocado, chives and combined remaining ingredients; toss gently to combine.

on the table in 30 minutes
serves 4 **per serving** 40.0g total fat (11.8g saturated fat); 3164kJ (757 cal); 68.6g carbohydrate; 28.0g protein; 5.8g fibre

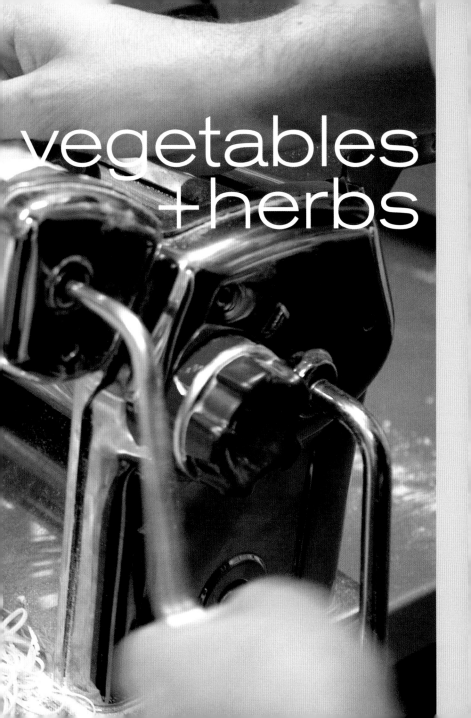

vegetables
+herbs

Spaghetti with tomato and white beans

⅓ cup (80ml) vegetable stock
1 small red onion (100g), chopped finely
1 clove garlic, crushed
1 cup (250ml) dry white wine
½ teaspoon white sugar
2 cups (500ml) bottled tomato pasta sauce
500g spaghetti
1 tablespoon coarsely chopped fresh oregano
2 tablespoons drained capers, chopped coarsely
½ cup (60g) seeded black olives, quartered
300g can white beans, rinsed, drained
2 tablespoons coarsely chopped fresh flat-leaf parsley

1 Heat half of the stock in medium saucepan, add onion and garlic;
cook, stirring, until onion is soft. Stir in wine, remaining stock, sugar
and sauce; bring to a boil. Reduce heat, simmer, uncovered, until sauce
thickens slightly.
2 Meanwhile, cook pasta in large saucepan of boiling water, uncovered,
until just tender; drain.
3 Stir remaining ingredients into sauce; cook, stirring, until hot. Serve
spaghetti with tomato and white beans.

on the table in 30 minutes
serves 4 **per serving** 2.9g total fat (0.5g saturated fat); 2479kJ (593 cal);
107.3g carbohydrate; 18.3g protein; 8.8g fibre
tip many varieties of already cooked white beans are available canned,
among them cannellini, butter and haricot beans; any of these are suitable
for this recipe.

Pasta with fresh tomato sauce

375g fresh lasagne sheets, sliced thickly
1 tablespoon olive oil
6 medium tomatoes (900g), peeled, seeded, chopped coarsely
¼ cup coarsely chopped fresh basil
2 cloves garlic, crushed
2 teaspoons red wine vinegar
1 fresh small red thai chilli, chopped finely
80g fetta cheese, crumbled

1 Cook pasta in large saucepan of boiling water, uncovered, until just tender; drain. Sprinkle half of the oil over pasta; toss gently to combine.
2 Meanwhile, place tomato, basil, garlic, remaining oil, vinegar and chilli in medium bowl; toss gently to combine.
3 Divide pasta among serving plates. Spoon tomato mixture over pasta; sprinkle with cheese.

on the table in 35 minutes
serves 4 **per serving** 9.6g total fat (3.7g saturated fat); 949kJ (227 cal); 25.0g carbohydrate; 8.3g protein; 3.1g fibre
tips to peel tomatoes, slice a cross in the bottom of tomato. Place tomatoes in large bowl of boiling water for 1 minute; drain. Rinse under cold water; peel. Fresh lasagne, available loose by weight from good delicatessens or in cryovac packages from supermarkets, take virtually no time at all to cook.

115

Pagli e fieno

2 teaspoons olive oil
5 green onions, sliced thinly
2 cloves garlic, crushed
500g button mushrooms, sliced thickly
1 tablespoon dry white wine
1¼ cups (310ml) cream
¼ cup coarsely chopped fresh flat-leaf parsley
150g fettuccine
150g spinach-flavoured fettuccine

1 Heat oil in medium saucepan; cook onion and garlic, stirring, until onion softens.
2 Add mushrooms to pan; cook, stirring, until just browned. Add wine and cream; bring to a boil. Reduce heat, simmer, uncovered, about 5 minutes or until sauce thickens slightly. Stir in parsley.
3 Meanwhle, cook both pastas in large saucepan of boiling water, uncovered, until just tender; drain.
4 Place pasta in large warmed bowl with sauce; toss gently to combine.

on the table in 25 minutes
serves 4 **per serving** 37.1g total fat (22.6g saturated fat); 2650kJ (634 cal); 56.3g carbohydrate; 15.0g protein; 6.7g fibre

Pappardelle with roasted tomato, spinach and ricotta

¼ cup (60ml) balsamic vinegar
3 cloves garlic, crushed
4 medium tomatoes (600g), cut into eight wedges
375g pappardelle pasta
100g baby spinach leaves
2 tablespoons olive oil
200g ricotta cheese

1 Preheat oven to 200°C/180°C fan-forced.
2 Combine vinegar and garlic in small jug. Place tomato, in single layer, on oven tray; pour vinegar mixture over tomato. Roast, uncovered, about 25 minutes or until tomato is browned lightly and softened.
3 Meanwhile, cook pasta in large saucepan of boiling water, uncovered, until just tender; drain.
4 Place pasta, tomato, spinach and oil in large bowl. Break ricotta into about 3cm pieces; add to pasta mixture, toss gently to combine.

on the table in 35 minutes
serves 4 **per serving** 15.9g total fat (5.1g saturated fat); 2002kJ (479 cal); 64.9g carbohydrate; 16.5g protein; 4.1g fibre

Spaghettini with parsley pesto

375g spaghettini
1 cup firmly packed fresh flat-leaf parsley leaves
1 cup firmly packed fresh basil leaves
2 tablespoons toasted pine nuts
2 cloves garlic, quartered
2 tablespoons finely grated pecorino cheese
½ cup (125ml) olive oil
⅓ cup (25g) pecorino cheese flakes

1 Cook pasta in large saucepan of boiling water, uncovered, until just tender; drain.
2 Meanwhile, blend or process herbs, pine nuts, garlic and grated cheese until combined. With motor operating, gradually add half of the oil in thin stream until combined.
3 Combine pasta, pesto and the remaining oil in large saucepan; toss gently to combine. Serve sprinkled with cheese.

on the table in 25 minutes
serves 4 **per serving** 38.8g total fat (7.0g saturated fat); 3265kJ (781 cal); 85.9g carbohydrate; 19.3g protein; 5.7g fibre

Cherry tomato and spinach pasta

⅓ cup (80ml) olive oil
4 cloves garlic, crushed
250g cherry tomatoes
1 small red onion (100g), sliced thinly
375g elbow macaroni
100g baby spinach
2 tablespoons torn fresh basil leaves
½ cup (50g) toasted walnuts, chopped coarsely
½ cup (40g) parmesan cheese flakes

1 Heat 2 tablespoons of the oil in large frying pan, add garlic, tomatoes and onion; cook, stirring, until onion is softened.
2 Meanwhile, cook pasta in large saucepan of boiling water, uncovered, until just tender; drain.
3 Place tomato mixture and pasta in large serving bowl with remaining oil, spinach, basil and walnuts; toss gently to combine.
4 Serve topped with cheese.

on the table in 20 minutes
serves 4 **per serving** 31.4g total fat (5.4g saturated fat); 2654kJ (635 cal); 67.5g carbohydrate; 17.6g protein; 6.4g fibre

Penne arrabiata

1 tablespoon olive oil
2 medium brown onions (300g), chopped finely
5 cloves garlic, crushed
3 fresh small red thai chillies, chopped finely
2⅓ cups (580ml) bottled tomato pasta sauce
2 teaspoons balsamic vinegar
375g penne pasta
¼ cup (20g) finely grated parmesan cheese

1 Heat oil in large saucepan; cook onion, garlic and chilli, stirring, until onion softens. Add sauce and vinegar; bring to a boil. Reduce heat, simmer, uncovered, about 5 minutes or until sauce thickens slightly.
2 Meanwhile, cook pasta in large saucepan of boiling water, uncovered, until just tender; drain.
3 Combine pasta with sauce; sprinkle with cheese.

on the table in 25 minutes
serves 4 **per serving** 8.6g total fat (2.1g saturated fat); 2111kJ (505 cal); 85.5g carbohydrate; 16.2g protein; 8.0g fibre
tip place any leftover pasta and sauce in an oiled ovenproof dish, cover with mozzarella cheese; bake in 180°C/160°C fan-forced oven until heated through and cheese bubbles.

Spaghetti napoletana

2 teaspoons olive oil
1 small brown onion (80g), chopped finely
3 cloves garlic, crushed
850g canned tomatoes
¼ cup coarsely chopped fresh basil
⅓ cup coarsely chopped fresh flat-leaf parsley
375g spaghetti

1 Heat oil in large saucepan, add onion and garlic; cook, stirring, until onion softens.
2 Add undrained crushed tomatoes to pan; bring to a boil. Reduce heat, simmer, uncovered, about 20 minutes or until reduced by about a third. Stir in basil and parsley.
3 Meanwhile, cook pasta in large saucepan of boiling water, uncovered, until just tender; drain.
4 Serve pasta topped with sauce.

on the table in 30 minutes
serves 4 **per serving** 3.8g total fat (0.5g saturated fat); 1630kJ (390 cal); 71.9g carbohydrate; 12.7g protein; 6.6g fibre

Spring greens and goat cheese pasta

Casarecce is a short, slightly tubular pasta like a twisted scroll.

400g frozen broad beans
500g casarecce pasta
⅓ cup (80ml) olive oil
2 small zucchini (180g), sliced thinly
1 clove garlic, crushed
150g shelled fresh peas
150g goat cheese, crumbled
½ cup loosely packed fresh mint leaves
lemon and garlic crumbs
40g butter
1 tablespoon olive oil
1 clove garlic, crushed
1 teaspoon finely grated lemon rind
1 cup (70g) coarse fresh breadcrumbs

1 Place broad beans in large heatproof bowl, cover with boiling water; stand 10 minutes. Drain. When cool enough to handle, peel grey outer shell from beans; discard shells.
2 Meanwhile, cook pasta in large saucepan of boiling water, uncovered, until just tender; drain. Return to pan, cover to keep warm.
3 Heat oil in large saucepan, add zucchini, garlic and peas; cook, stirring, about 5 minutes or until zucchini is almost browned. Add broad beans, cook 1 minute.
4 Make lemon and garlic crumbs.
5 Combine pasta, zucchini mixture, cheese and mint leaves. Top with lemon and garlic crumbs.
lemon and garlic crumbs heat butter and oil in medium frying pan, add garlic, rind and breadcrumbs; cook, stirring, until breadcrumbs are golden and crisp.

on the table in 35 minutes
serves 4 **per serving** 39.6g total fat (12.9g saturated fat); 3984kJ (953 cal); 110.8g carbohydrate; 29.8g protein; 16.7g fibre

Ravioli with pumpkin and sage sauce

1 tablespoon olive oil
8 large fresh sage leaves
500g pumpkin, cut into 1cm cubes
4 green onions, chopped coarsely
1 tablespoon thinly shredded fresh sage
750g ravioli
1 tablespoon balsamic vinegar
¾ cup (180ml) cream
¾ cup (180ml) vegetable stock

1 Heat oil in large frying pan, add sage leaves; cook, stirring gently, until bright green and crisp. Drain on absorbent paper.
2 Cook pumpkin in same pan, uncovered, stirring occasionally, about 15 minutes or until browned lightly and just tender. Add onion and shredded sage; cook, stirring, 1 minute. Remove from pan; cover to keep warm.
3 Meanwhile, cook pasta in large saucepan of boiling water, uncovered, until just tender; drain. Cover to keep warm.
4 Place vinegar, cream and stock in same cleaned frying pan; bring to a boil. Reduce heat, simmer, uncovered, 5 minutes. Add pumpkin mixture; cook, stirring, over low heat until sauce is heated through.
5 Serve pasta topped with sauce and fried sage leaves.

on the table in 35 minutes
serves 4 **per serving** 34.0g total fat (17.7g saturated fat); 2178kJ (521 cal); 34.5g carbohydrate; 17.8g protein; 4.3g fibre
tip we used a roasted vegetable ravioli, but you can use any variety of ravioli or other filled pasta you like.

Penne with cherry tomatoes and salami

500g penne pasta
150g sliced hot salami
500g cherry tomatoes
2 cloves garlic, crushed
⅓ cup loosely packed fresh parsley leaves
¼ cup loosely packed fresh oregano leaves
200g baby bocconcini cheese, halved
2 tablespoons olive oil

1 Cook pasta in large saucepan of boiling water, uncovered, until just tender; drain.
2 Meanwhile, cook salami in large frying pan, stirring, until crisp; drain on absorbent paper.
3 Cook tomatoes in same pan, stirring, until softened. Add garlic; cook, stirring, until fragrant.
4 Place hot pasta, salami, tomato mixture in large bowl with herbs, cheese and oil; toss gently to combine.

on the table in 30 minutes
serves 4 **per serving** 32.4g total fat (11.2g saturated fat); 3290kJ (787 cal); 88.7g carbohydrate; 31.6g protein; 6.6g fibre

Roasted kumara and parmesan with curly lasagne

1 large kumara (500g)
2 tablespoons olive oil
250g curly lasagne
1 cup (80g) parmesan cheese flakes
250g rocket leaves, torn
¼ cup (60ml) balsamic vinegar
¼ cup (60ml) olive oil, extra
1 clove garlic, crushed

1 Preheat oven to 240°C/220°C fan-forced.
2 Halve kumara lengthways; slice halves into 5mm pieces. Combine kumara and oil in large baking dish; roast, uncovered, about 25 minutes or until tender.
3 Meanwhile, break pasta roughly lengthways. Cook pasta in large saucepan of boiling water, uncovered, until just tender; drain.
4 Place pasta, kumara, cheese, rocket and combined remaining ingredients in large bowl; toss gently to combine.

on the table in 35 minutes
serves 4 as an entree **per serving** 30.0g total fat (7.3g saturated fat); 1914kJ (458 cal); 31.8g carbohydrate; 13.8g protein; 4.1g fibre

Tomato, olive and anchovy pasta

½ cup (125ml) olive oil
2 cloves garlic, crushed
1 teaspoon dried oregano leaves
6 drained anchovy fillets, chopped finely
4 medium vine-ripened tomatoes (760g), chopped
2 tablespoons drained baby capers
½ cup (80g) seeded black olives, halved
500g garganelli pasta

1 Heat oil in large frying pan; cook garlic, oregano and anchovies, stirring, until fragrant. Add tomato, capers and olives; cook, stirring, until heated through.
2 Meanwhile, cook pasta in large saucepan of boiling water, uncovered, until just tender; drain. Return to pan.
3 Add sauce to pasta; toss gently to combine.

on the table in 20 minutes
serves 4 **per serving** 30.6g total fat (4.4g saturated fat); 3085kJ (738 cal); 94.1g carbohydrate; 17.7g protein; 7.0g fibre

Fresh tomato and chilli pasta

500g penne pasta
⅓ cup (80ml) olive oil
1 clove garlic, crushed
1 fresh small red thai chilli, chopped finely
4 medium ripe tomatoes (800g), chopped
1 cup chopped fresh flat-leaf parsley
½ cup (40g) parmesan cheese flakes

1 Cook pasta in large saucepan of boiling water, uncovered, until just tender; drain.
2 Meanwhile, heat oil in large frying pan, add garlic and chilli; cook, stirring, about 1 minute or until fragrant. Add tomato and parsley; remove from heat.
3 Add sauce mixture to pasta; toss gently to combine.
4 Serve topped with cheese.

on the table in 20 minutes
serves 4 **per serving** 23.1g total fat (4.9g saturated fat); 2767kJ (662 cal); 89.2g carbohydrate; 20.2g protein; 7.4g fibre

Creamy bow ties with fried zucchini

375g bow tie pasta
2 tablespoons olive oil
3 cloves garlic, crushed
6 small zucchini (540g), grated coarsely
2 teaspoons finely grated lemon rind
1 tablespoon finely chopped fresh flat-leaf parsley
3 green onions, sliced thinly
½ cup (40g) finely grated parmesan cheese
300ml cream

1 Cook pasta in large saucepan of boiling water, uncovered, until just tender; drain.
2 Meanwhile, heat oil in large frying pan, add garlic; cook, stirring, about 2 minutes or until fragrant. Add zucchini; cook, stirring, 2 minutes.
3 Combine rind, parsley, onion and cheese in small bowl.
4 Add cream and hot pasta to zucchini mixture; stir gently over low heat until heated through. Serve immediately, topped with cheese mixture.

on the table in 30 minutes
serves 4 **per serving** 46.3g total fat (25.0g saturated fat); 3227kJ (772 cal); 68.8g carbohydrate; 17.7g protein; 5.9g fibre

Linguine with beans, potatoes and basil pesto

250g green beans, cut into 5cm lengths
2 medium potatoes (400g), sliced thinly lengthways
500g linguine
1¼ cups (100g) pecorino cheese flakes
basil pesto
1 cup firmly packed fresh basil leaves
¼ cup (20g) finely grated pecorino cheese
¼ cup (40g) toasted pine nuts
2 cloves garlic, crushed
½ cup (125ml) olive oil

1 Boil, steam or microwave beans and potato, separately, until just tender; drain.
2 Meanwhile, cook pasta in large saucepan of boiling water, uncovered, until just tender; drain, reserving ½ cup of the cooking liquid.
3 Make basil pesto; stir in reserved cooking liquid.
4 Place beans, potato and pasta in large bowl with pesto and cheese; toss gently to combine.
basil pesto blend or process ingredients until it forms a coarse paste.

on the table in 35 minutes
serves 4 **per serving** 45.3g total fat (9.9g saturated fat); 3867kJ (925 cal); 101.4g carbohydrate; 27.3g protein; 10.3g fibre

Fettuccine with summer tomato sauce

375g fettuccine
2 large tomatoes (500g), chopped finely
1 medium white onion (150g), chopped finely
6 seeded green olives, chopped finely
1 tablespoon capers, drained, chopped finely
2 teaspoons finely chopped fresh oregano
⅓ cup finely chopped fresh flat-leaf parsley
2 cloves garlic, crushed
¼ cup (60ml) olive oil

1 Cook pasta in large saucepan of boiling water, uncovered, until just tender; drain.
2 Meanwhile, place remaining ingredients in large bowl; mix well.
3 Add pasta to tomato mixture; toss gently to combine.

on the table in 20 minutes
serves 4 **per serving** 15.1g total fat (2.2g saturated fat); 2044kJ (489 cal); 72.2g carbohydrate; 12.6g protein; 5.8g fibre

Risoni with mushrooms, zucchini and green onions

500g risoni pasta
1 tablespoon olive oil
60g butter
500g zucchini, sliced thinly
300g button mushrooms, sliced thinly
2 cloves garlic, crushed
1 tablespoon coarsely chopped fresh oregano
1 tablespoon lemon juice
1 tablespoon red wine vinegar
200g green onions, sliced thinly
½ cup (40g) coarsely grated parmesan cheese

1 Cook pasta in large saucepan of boiling water, uncovered, until just tender; drain.
2 Meanwhile, heat oil with half of the butter in large frying pan; cook zucchini, stirring, until tender.
3 Add remaining butter to pan with mushrooms, garlic and oregano; cook, stirring, 2 minutes then stir in juice and vinegar. Remove from heat; stir in onion and cheese.
4 Place pasta and zucchini mixture in large serving bowl; toss gently to combine.

on the table in 30 minutes
serves 4 **per serving** 22.2g total fat (11.1g saturated fat); 2817kJ (674 cal); 90.2g carbohydrate; 23.1g protein; 9.4g fibre
tip risoni is a small rice-shaped pasta that can be served similarly to orzo or rice in salads and soups.

Penne puttanesca

500g penne pasta
⅓ cup (80ml) olive oil
3 cloves garlic, crushed
1 teaspoon dried chilli flakes
5 medium tomatoes (950g), chopped coarsely
1¼ cups (200g) seeded kalamata olives
8 anchovy fillets, drained, chopped coarsely
⅓ cup (65g) rinsed drained capers
⅓ cup coarsely chopped fresh flat-leaf parsley
2 tablespoons finely shredded fresh basil

1 Cook pasta in large saucepan of boiling water, uncovered, until just tender; drain.
2 Meanwhile, heat oil in large frying pan; cook garlic, stirring, until fragrant. Add chilli and tomato; cook, stirring, 5 minutes. Add remaining ingredients; cook, stirring occasionally, about 5 minutes or until sauce thickens slightly.
3 Add pasta to puttanesca sauce; toss gently to combine.

on the table in 25 minutes
serves 4 **per serving** 20.9g total fat (3.0g saturated fat); 2905kJ (695 cal); 102.6g carbohydrate; 19.1g protein; 8.5g fibre

Penne with matriciana sauce

1 tablespoon olive oil
1 medium brown onion (150g), chopped finely
6 rashers rindless bacon (360g), sliced thinly
2 large tomatoes (500g), peeled, chopped coarsely
1 fresh small red thai chilli, chopped finely
375g penne pasta

1 Heat oil in large frying pan; cook onion and bacon, stirring, over medium heat about 5 minutes or until onion is soft. Drain off excess fat. Add tomato and chilli; mix well. Simmer gently, uncovered, 5 minutes, stirring occasionally.
2 Meanwhile, cook pasta in large saucepan of boiling water, uncovered, until just tender; drain.
3 Combine sauce and pasta.

on the table in 30 minutes
serves 4 **per serving** 8.8g total fat (1.9g saturated fat); 1940kJ (464 cal); 68.6g carbohydrate; 24.1g protein; 5.1g fibre
tip pancetta can be substituted for bacon in this recipe.

151

Rigatoni with eggplant sauce

¼ cup (60ml) olive oil
1 medium brown onion (150g), chopped finely
2 trimmed celery stalks (200g), chopped finely
1 clove garlic, crushed
2 tablespoons brandy
1 medium eggplant (300g), sliced thinly
2⅓ cups (580ml) bottled tomato pasta sauce
½ cup (140g) tomato paste
½ cup (125ml) water
375g rigatoni pasta
¼ cup (20g) finely grated parmesan cheese

1 Heat oil in large saucepan; cook onion, celery and garlic, stirring, until onion softens. Add brandy; cook, stirring, until brandy evaporates. Add eggplant; cook, stirring, until eggplant is tender.
2 Stir in sauce, paste and the water; bring to a boil. Reduce heat, simmer, uncovered, about 10 minutes or until sauce thickens slightly.
3 Meanwhile, cook pasta in large saucepan of boiling water, uncovered, until just tender; drain.
4 Place pasta and half the eggplant sauce in large bowl; toss gently to combine. Divide pasta among serving plates; top each with remaining sauce. Serve with cheese.

on the table in 30 minutes
serves 4 **per serving** 18.0g total fat (3.3g saturated fat); 2650kJ (634 cal); 89.2g carbohydrate; 17.7g protein; 10.9g fibre

Spaghetti with zucchini, tomato and ricotta

500g spaghetti
¼ cup (60ml) olive oil
4 medium zucchini (480g), cut into 5cm lengths
3 cloves garlic, sliced thinly
500g cherry tomatoes
100g baby rocket leaves
1¼ cups (250g) ricotta cheese, crumbled

1 Cook pasta in large saucepan of boiling water, uncovered, until just tender; drain.
2 Meanwhile, heat oil in large frying pan; cook zucchini, stirring, until just tender. Add garlic and tomatoes; cook, stirring occasionally, until tomatoes split and soften.
3 Place pasta, zucchini mixture and rocket in large bowl; toss gently to combine. Serve topped with cheese.

on the table in 25 minutes
serves 4 **per serving** 22.8g total fat (6.7g saturated fat); 2863kJ (685 cal); 91.1g carbohydrate; 24.0g protein; 8.3g fibre

Spirals with crisp salami and tomato sauce

500g spiral pasta
1 tablespoon olive oil
200g thinly sliced danish salami
2 cloves garlic, crushed
3 small zucchini (280g), sliced thinly
1 teaspoon dried chilli flakes
700g bottled tomato pasta sauce
1¼ cups (150g) seeded green olives
1 cup coarsely chopped fresh flat-leaf parsley

1 Cook pasta in large saucepan of boiling water, uncovered, until just tender; drain.
2 Meanwhile, heat half of the oil in medium frying pan; cook salami, stirring, until crisp. Drain on absorbent paper; cut slices into strips.
3 Heat remaining oil in same cleaned pan; cook garlic and zucchini, stirring, about 2 minutes or until zucchini is just tender. Stir in salami with chilli, sauce and olives; cook, stirring, until heated through.
4 Place pasta and tomato sauce in large bowl with parsley; toss gently to combine.

on the table in 30 minutes
serves 4 **per serving** 27.9g total fat (7.8g saturated fat); 3486kJ (834 cal); 112.0g carbohydrate; 27.7g protein; 9.8g fibre
tips Danish salami is a smoked, delicately spiced salami; again, you can use another variety if you wish.

Fettuccine with rocket pesto and fresh tomato salsa

500g fettuccine
8 cloves garlic, quartered
½ cup coarsely chopped fresh basil
120g rocket, chopped coarsely
⅔ cup (160ml) olive oil
½ cup (40g) finely grated parmesan cheese
3 medium tomatoes (570g), chopped coarsely
2 tablespoons lemon juice
2 fresh small red thai chillies, sliced thinly
⅓ cup (50g) toasted pine nuts

1 Cook pasta in large saucepan of boiling water, uncovered, until just tender; drain.
2 Meanwhile, blend or process garlic, basil, rocket and oil until smooth.
3 Place pasta and pesto in large saucepan with cheese, tomato, juice and chilli; cook, stirring, until hot. Add nuts; toss gently to combine.

on the table in 30 minutes
serves 4 **per serving** 50.3g total fat (8.0g saturated fat); 3833kJ (917 cal); 90.2g carbohydrate; 22.2g protein; 8.1g fibre
tip you could substitute baby spinach leaves for the rocket, if you like, for a milder flavoured pesto.

Ricotta and spinach ravioli with pumpkin sauce

¼ cup (60ml) olive oil
1 small brown onion (80g), chopped finely
1 clove garlic, crushed
600g pumpkin, sliced thinly
1½ cups (375ml) chicken stock
½ teaspoon ground nutmeg
½ cup (125ml) cream
½ cup (125ml) hot water
600g fresh spinach and ricotta ravioli
⅓ cup (50g) toasted pine nuts
2 tablespoons coarsely chopped fresh chives

1 Heat half of the oil in large frying pan; cook onion and garlic, stirring, until onion softens. Remove from pan.
2 Heat remaining oil in same pan; cook pumpkin, in batches, until browned lightly. Return pumpkin and onion mixture to pan with stock and nutmeg; cook, stirring, until liquid is absorbed. Blend or process pumpkin mixture with cream and the hot water until smooth. Return to pan; stir, over low heat, until heated through.
3 Meanwhile, cook pasta in large saucepan of boiling water, uncovered, until just tender; drain.
4 Serve pasta with pumpkin sauce, sprinkled with pine nuts and chives.

on the table in 35 minutes
serves 4 **per serving** 42.3g total fat (13.6g saturated fat); 2391kJ (572 cal); 31.6g carbohydrate; 17.5g protein; 4.8g fibre

Pasta with eggplant, tomato and bocconcini

2 tablespoons olive oil
1 large eggplant (500g), chopped
1 medium red onion (170g), chopped finely
2 cloves garlic, crushed
425g can crushed tomatoes
½ teaspoons dried chilli flakes
2 tablespoons cream
¼ cup loosely packed fresh basil leaves
500g tortiglioni pasta
180g cherry bocconcini cheese, halved
¼ cup (20g) parmesan cheese flakes

1 Heat oil in large saucepan; cook eggplant, stirring, about 5 minutes or until browned lightly. Add onion and garlic; cook, stirring, until soft. Add undrained tomatoes and chilli; cook, covered, stirring occasionally, 10 minutes.
2 Stir cream and basil into eggplant mixture.
3 Meanwhile, cook pasta in large saucepan of boiling water, uncovered, until just tender; drain.
4 Toss pasta with bocconcini, eggplant mixture and half of the parmesan. Serve topped with remaining parmesan.

on the table in 35 minutes
serves 4 **per serving** 21.8g total fat (8.5g saturated fat); 2934kJ (702 cal); 94.4g carbohydrate; 26.7g protein; 9.2g fibre

Marinated vegetable pasta

2 cloves garlic, crushed
290g jar mixed antipasto, drained, chopped coarsely
340g jar marinated artichokes, drained, quartered
⅓ cup (80ml) vegetable stock
⅓ cup (80ml) dry red wine
700g bottled tomato pasta sauce
500g rigatoni pasta
½ cup coarsely chopped fresh basil
½ cup (40g) parmesan cheese flakes

1 Cook garlic, antipasto and artichoke in large frying pan, stirring,
3 minutes. Stir in stock, wine and sauce; bring to a boil. Reduce heat,
simmer, uncovered, about 5 minutes or until sauce thickens slightly.
2 Meanwhile, cook pasta in large saucepan of boiling water, uncovered,
until just tender; drain.
3 Add pasta and basil to sauce; toss gently to combine. Divide pasta
among serving bowls; top with cheese.

on the table in 25 minutes
serves 4 **per serving** 11.7g total fat (3.7g saturated fat); 3620kJ
(866 cal); 139.7g carbohydrate; 33.6g protein; 23.4g fibre

Chilli and garlic spaghettini with breadcrumbs

375g spaghettini
⅓ cup (80ml) olive oil
50g butter
4 cloves garlic, crushed
4 fresh small red thai chillies, chopped finely
2 cups (140g) stale breadcrumbs
½ cup coarsely chopped fresh flat-leaf parsley
2 teaspoons finely grated lemon rind

1 Cook pasta in large saucepan of boiling water, uncovered, until just tender; drain.
2 Meanwhile, heat half of the oil and butter in large frying pan; cook garlic, chilli and breadcrumbs, stirring, until breadcrumbs are browned lightly.
3 Place pasta and breadcrumb mixture in large bowl with parsley, rind and remaining oil; toss gently to combine.

on the table in 20 minutes
serves 4 **per serving** 30.8g total fat (9.7g saturated fat); 2939kJ (703 cal); 88.1g carbohydrate; 15.7g protein; 5.1g fibre

Roasted pumpkin and fetta pasta

1kg pumpkin, chopped coarsely
2 teaspoons caraway seeds
⅓ cup (80ml) olive oil
375g linguine
⅓ cup (50g) toasted pine nuts
2 tablespoons coarsely chopped fresh flat-leaf parsley
200g fetta cheese, crumbled
¼ cup (60ml) lemon juice
1 clove garlic, crushed
2 tablespoons white wine vinegar

1 Preheat oven to 240°C/220°C fan-forced.
2 Place pumpkin, seeds and 2 tablespoons of the oil in large shallow baking dish; toss to combine. Roast, uncovered, about 20 minutes or until pumpkin is brown and tender.
3 Meanwhile, cook pasta in large saucepan of boiling water, uncovered, until just tender; drain.
4 Combine pasta and pumpkin mixture in large bowl with pine nuts, parsley and cheese. Drizzle with combined juice, garlic, vinegar and remaining oil; toss gently to combine.

on the table in 35 minutes
serves 4 **per serving** 24.6g total fat (9.3g saturated fat); 2721kJ (651 cal); 78.3g carbohydrate; 25.5g protein; 6.5g fibre
tip linguine, also known as flat spaghetti or little tongues, are long, narrow, flat noodles. Bavette or spaghetti are suitable substitutes.

Angel hair pasta with peas and ricotta

375g angel hair pasta
150g sugar snap peas, trimmed
150g snow peas, trimmed
½ cup (60g) frozen peas
1 tablespoon olive oil
1 medium red onion (170g), sliced thinly
2 cloves garlic, crushed
2 tablespoons drained baby capers, rinsed
½ cup (125ml) lemon juice
½ cup coarsely chopped fresh mint
½ cup coarsely chopped fresh flat-leaf parsley
200g ricotta cheese, crumbled

1 Cook pasta in large saucepan of boiling water, uncovered, until just tender; drain.
2 Meanwhile, boil, steam or microwave peas until just tender; drain. Rinse under cold water; drain.
3 Heat oil in large saucepan; cook onion, garlic and capers, stirring, 2 minutes. Add pasta; cook, stirring, 4 minutes. Place pasta mixture, peas, juice and herbs in large bowl; toss gently.
4 Serve pasta topped with cheese.

on the table in 30 minutes
serves 4 **per serving** 10.4g total fat (3.7g saturated fat); 1990kJ (476 cal); 73.9g carbohydrate; 20.1g protein; 7.5g fibre

171

Asparagus, bacon and cheese pasta

500g tortiglioni pasta
500g asparagus, trimmed, chopped coarsely
5 rashers rindless bacon (300g), sliced thinly
1 clove garlic, crushed
50g butter, chopped
½ cup (40g) finely grated parmesan cheese
½ cup (50g) finely grated mozzarella cheese
⅓ cup (80ml) cream
¼ cup coarsely chopped fresh flat-leaf parsley

1 Cook pasta in large saucepan of boiling water, uncovered, until just tender; drain.
2 Meanwhile, boil, steam or microwave asparagus until just tender; drain.
3 Cook bacon in large heated frying pan, stirring, until crisp. Add garlic; cook, stirring, until fragrant.
4 Place pasta, asparagus and bacon mixture in large bowl with butter, cheeses and cream; toss gently to combine. Serve sprinkled with parsley.

on the table in 35 minutes
serves 4 **per serving** 31.2g total fat (17.9g saturated fat); 3240kJ (775 cal); 90g carbohydrate; 32.7g protein; 7.8g fibre

Penne with char-grilled capsicum and pine nuts

2 large red capsicums (700g)
375g penne pasta
2 tablespoons olive oil
2 cloves garlic, crushed
½ cup (80g) toasted pine nuts
2 fresh small red thai chillies, chopped finely
¼ cup (60ml) lemon juice
100g baby rocket leaves
100g fetta cheese, crumbled

1 Quarter capsicums; discard seeds and membranes. Roast under grill or in very hot oven, skin-side up, until skin blisters and blackens. Cover capsicum pieces in plastic or paper for 5 minutes, peel away skin then slice thinly.
2 Meanwhile, cook pasta in large saucepan of boiling water, uncovered, until just tender; drain.
3 Heat oil in large frying pan; cook garlic, nuts and chilli, stirring, about 2 minutes or until fragrant. Add capsicum and juice; stir until hot.
4 Place pasta and capsicum mixture in large bowl with rocket and cheese; toss gently to combine.

on the table in 35 minutes
serves 4 **per serving** 30.5g total fat (6.2g saturated fat); 2755kJ (659 cal); 74.4g carbohydrate; 21g protein; 8.2g fibre

Pappardelle with chilli and semi-dried tomato sauce

2 medium brown onions (300g), chopped coarsely
2 cloves garlic, quartered
1 cup (150g) semi-dried tomatoes in oil, drained
¼ cup (70g) tomato paste
2 fresh small red thai chillies, chopped finely
2 cups (500ml) beef stock
375g pappardelle pasta
¼ cup coarsely chopped fresh flat-leaf parsley

1 Blend or process onion, garlic, tomatoes, paste and chilli until mixture forms a paste.
2 Heat large frying pan; cook tomato mixture, stirring, 5 minutes. Stir in stock, bring to a boil. Reduce heat, simmer sauce, uncovered, about 10 minutes or until thickened slightly.
3 Meanwhile, cook pasta in large saucepan of boiling water, uncovered, until just tender; drain.
4 Gently toss pasta through sauce; sprinkle with parsley.

on the table in 35 minutes
serves 4 **per serving** 3.2g total fat (0.6g saturated fat); 1935kJ (463 cal); 84.0g carbohydrate; 18.0g protein; 10.8g fibre

Spaghetti with rocket, parmesan and pine nuts

500g spaghetti
⅓ cup (80ml) olive oil
2 cloves garlic, crushed
2 fresh small red thai chillies, chopped finely
½ cup (80g) toasted pine nuts
1 cup (80g) parmesan cheese flakes
200g baby rocket leaves

1 Cook pasta in large saucepan of boiling water, uncovered, until just tender; drain.
2 Heat oil in small saucepan; cook garlic and chilli, stirring, about 30 seconds or until garlic just softens and is fragrant (do not brown the garlic).
3 Place hot pasta and oil mixture in large bowl with pine nuts, cheese and rocket; toss to combine.

on the table in 20 minutes
serves 4 **per serving** 40.5g total fat (7.8g saturated fat); 3461kJ (828 cal); 87.5g carbohydrate; 25.6g protein; 6.2g fibre

Spaghetti with anchovies, olives and rocket

375g spaghetti
400g grape tomatoes
¼ cup (60ml) olive oil
4 drained anchovy fillets, chopped
2 cloves garlic, crushed
2 fresh long red chillies, sliced thinly
100g black olives, seeded, halved
100g wild rocket leaves

1 Cook pasta in large saucepan of boiling water, uncovered, until just tender; drain, return pasta to pan.
2 Meanwhile, halve 200g of the tomatoes.
3 Heat 1 tablespoon of the oil in medium frying pan; cook anchovies, garlic and chilli, stirring, until soft and fragrant. Add tomatoes, stir until combined.
4 Toss tomato mixture through spaghetti with olives, rocket and remaining oil.

on the table in 30 minutes
serves 4 **per serving** 15.4g total fat (2.2g saturated fat); 2044kJ (489 cal); 71.4g carbohydrate; 12.9g protein; 5.6g fibre

Roast tomato with basil and olive oil

8 medium egg tomatoes (600g), chopped coarsely
2 cloves garlic, crushed
¼ cup (60ml) olive oil
500g penne pasta
½ cup finely shredded fresh basil leaves

1 Preheat oven to 220°C/200°C fan-forced.
2 Combine tomato, garlic and oil in large baking dish; roast, uncovered, about 10 minutes or until tomato softens and browns slightly.
3 Meanwhile, cook pasta in large saucepan of boiling water, uncovered, until just tender; drain.
4 Place tomato mixture and pasta in large bowl with basil; toss gently to combine.

on the table in 25 minutes
serves 4 **per serving** 15.2g total fat (2.2g saturated fat); 2373kJ (569 cal); 88.3g carbohydrate; 15.7g protein; 6.3g fibre

Risoni with spinach and semi-dried tomatoes

30g butter
2 medium brown onions (300g), chopped finely
3 cloves garlic, crushed
500g risoni pasta
1 litre (4 cups) chicken stock
½ cup (125ml) dry white wine
150g semi-dried tomatoes, halved
100g baby spinach leaves
⅓ cup (25g) finely grated parmesan cheese

1 Melt butter in large saucepan; cook onion and garlic, stirring, until onion softens. Add risoni; stir to coat in butter mixture.
2 Stir in stock and wine; bring to a boil. Reduce to medium heat; simmer, stirring, until liquid is absorbed and risoni is just tender. Gently stir in tomato, spinach and cheese.

on the table in 30 minutes
serves 4 **per serving** 22.2g total fat (11.1g saturated fat); 2817kJ (674 cal); 90.2g carbohydrate; 23.1g protein; 9.4g fibre

Roasted capsicum, goat cheese and walnut pasta salad

375g large spiral pasta
2 medium red capsicums (400g)
2 medium yellow capsicums (400g)
150g goat cheese, crumbled
⅓ cup (35g) toasted walnuts, chopped coarsely
½ cup loosely packed fresh basil leaves
¼ cup (60ml) red wine vinegar
⅓ cup (80ml) olive oil
1 clove garlic, crushed
2 teaspoons wholegrain mustard

1 Cook pasta in large saucepan of boiling water, uncovered, until just tender; drain. Rinse under cold water; drain.
2 Meanwhile, quarter capsicums, remove and discard seeds and membranes. Roast under grill or in very hot oven, skin-side up, until skin blisters and blackens. Cover capsicum pieces with plastic or paper for 5 minutes, peel away skin; slice capsicum thickly.
3 Place pasta and capsicum in large bowl with cheese, walnuts, basil and combined remaining ingredients; toss gently to combine.

on the table in 35 minutes
serves 4 **per serving** 31.5g total fat (7.0g saturated fat); 2730kJ (653 cal); 70.0g carbohydrate; 19.4g protein; 5.7g fibre
tip fetta or any soft, crumbly cheese can be used instead of the goat cheese, and toasted pecan halves make a nice change from walnuts.

Pesto spaghettini

3 cloves garlic, peeled
⅓ cup (55g) toasted pine nuts
½ cup (40g) coarsely chopped parmesan cheese
3 cups (70g) lightly packed fresh basil leaves
½ cup (125ml) olive oil
500g spaghettini

1 Process garlic, pine nuts and cheese until chopped finely. With motor still operating, add basil then oil in a thin stream until combined.
2 Meanwhile, cook pasta in large saucepan of boiling water until just tender; drain, reserving 1 tablespoon of the cooking liquid. Return pasta to pan.
3 Add enough of the pesto and the reserved cooking liquid to coat the pasta lightly; toss gently to combine.

on the table in 20 minutes
serves 4 **per serving** 42.8g total fat (6.9g saturated fat); 3440kJ (823 cal); 86.4g carbohydrate; 20.1g protein; 5.9g fibre

Spaghetti with oil and garlic

500g spaghetti
⅓ cup (80ml) olive oil
3 cloves garlic, crushed
2 tablespoons finely chopped fresh flat-leaf parsley

1 Cook pasta in large saucepan of boiling water, uncovered, until just tender; drain.
2 Meanwhile, heat oil in large frying pan; cook garlic, gently, until golden brown. Add parsley. Combine sauce and pasta.

on the table in 15 minutes
serves 4 **per serving** 19.6g total fat (2.8g saturated fat); 2454kJ (587 cal); 85.5g carbohydrate; 14.2g protein; 4.6g fibre

Penne, roast capsicum and baby vegetables in burnt butter sauce

2 medium red capsicums (400g)
375g penne pasta
200g baby corn, halved lengthways
200g green beans, trimmed
100g butter
2 cloves garlic, crushed
2 tablespoons coarsely chopped fresh oregano

1 Quarter capsicums, remove and discard seeds and membranes. Roast under grill or in very hot oven, skin-side up, until skin blisters and blackens. Cover capsicum pieces with plastic or paper for 5 minutes; peel away skin, slice capsicum thinly.
2 Meanwhile, cook pasta in large saucepan of boiling water, uncovered, until just tender; drain.
3 Boil, steam or microwave corn and beans, separately, until just tender; drain.
4 Melt butter in small saucepan; cook, stirring, about 3 minutes or until browned. Remove from heat; stir in garlic and oregano.
5 Place capsicum, pasta, corn and beans in large bowl with burnt butter mixture; toss gently to combine.

on the table in 35 minutes
serves 4 **per serving** 22.4g total fat (13.7g saturated fat); 2458kJ (588 cal); 77.0g carbohydrate; 15.3g protein; 7.9g fibre

Mixed-mushroom orecchiette

1 tablespoon olive oil
1 medium brown onion (150g), chopped finely
2 cloves garlic, crushed
250g button mushrooms, sliced thickly
250g swiss brown mushrooms, sliced thickly
250g flat mushrooms, sliced thickly
250g spreadable cream cheese
½ cup (125ml) chicken stock
375g orecchiette pasta
½ teaspoon cracked black pepper
2 tablespoons coarsely chopped fresh flat-leaf parsley

1 Heat oil in large frying pan; cook onion and garlic, stirring, until onion softens. Add mushrooms; cook, stirring, until browned and tender. Add cream cheese and stock; cook over low heat, stirring, until cheese melts and mixture is hot.
2 Meanwhile, cook pasta in large saucepan of boiling water, uncovered, until just tender; drain.
3 Add pasta to mushroom sauce, stir in pepper and parsley; toss gently to combine.

on the table in 25 minutes
serves 4 **per serving** 27.0g total fat (14.2g saturated fat); 2629kJ (629 cal); 68.5g carbohydrate; 23.6g protein; 6.8g fibre

Fettuccine with mushrooms and chilli

2 tablespoons olive oil
500g button mushrooms, sliced thinly
2 fresh large mild red chillies, sliced thinly
1 clove garlic, crushed
500g fettuccine
⅓ cup (80ml) olive oil, extra
100g baby spinach leaves

1 Heat oil in large frying pan; cook mushrooms, stirring, 10 minutes or until tender. Add chilli and garlic, cook, stirring, until fragrant.
2 Meanwhile, cook pasta in large saucepan of boiling water, uncovered, until just tender. Drain, reserving ⅓ cup (80ml) of the cooking liquid.
3 Place mushroom mixture and pasta in large bowl with extra oil, spinach and reserved cooking liquid; toss gently to combine.

on the table in 25 minutes
serves 4 **per serving** 29.2g total fat (4.1g saturated fat); 2926kJ (700 cal); 85.9g carbohydrate; 19.2g protein; 8.1g fibre

Agnolotti in sage and pumpkin puree

Similar to ravioli, agnolotti are tiny pillows of pasta stuffed with one of any manner of different fillings. You can buy these already made, sold in cryovac packages, in the refrigerated section of your supermarket or fresh from specialty pasta makers.

1 teaspoon olive oil
1 small leek (200g), chopped finely
2 cloves garlic, crushed
400g peeled pumpkin, chopped
½ cup (125ml) buttermilk
½ cup (125ml) cream
½ cup (125ml) vegetable stock
750g ricotta and spinach agnolotti pasta
vegetable oil, for shallow-frying
1 cup loosely packed fresh sage leaves
2 egg yolks, beaten lightly
¼ cup (20g) finely grated parmesan cheese

1 Heat olive oil in large frying pan; cook leek and garlic, stirring, until leek softens.
2 Boil, steam or microwave pumpkin until tender; drain. Blend or process, in batches, with buttermilk, cream and stock. Add pumpkin mixture to leek mixture; bring to a boil. Reduce heat, simmer, stirring, 10 minutes or until mixture slightly thickens.
3 Meanwhile, cook pasta in large saucepan of boiling water, uncovered, until just tender; drain.
4 Heat vegetable oil in small frying pan; fry sage until crisp, drain on absorbent paper.
5 Stir egg yolk and cheese into pumpkin mixture.
6 Place pasta and pumpkin mixture in large bowl; toss gently to combine. Crumble fried sage leaves; sprinkle over pasta.

on the table in 30 minutes
serves 4 **per serving** 34.7g total fat (19.9g saturated fat); 2353kJ (563 cal); 37.6g carbohydrate; 23.0g protein; 5.3g fibre

Angel hair pasta with rocket, tomato and fetta

375g angel hair pasta
200g fetta cheese, crumbled
¼ cup (60ml) olive oil
2 fresh small red thai chillies, chopped finely
2 tablespoons shredded fresh basil
¼ cup coarsely chopped fresh flat-leaf parsley
3 cloves garlic, crushed
3 medium tomatoes (570g), seeded, sliced thinly
250g rocket, chopped coarsely

1 Cook pasta in large saucepan of boiling water, uncovered, until just tender; drain.
2 Meanwhile, place cheese in large bowl with oil, chilli, herbs, garlic, tomato and rocket; toss to combine. Add pasta; toss gently to combine.

on the table in 20 minutes
serves 4 **per serving** 26.9g total fat (9.8g saturated fat); 2541kJ (608 cal); 66.8g carbohydrate; 21.8g protein; 5.3g fibre

Pasta primavera

375g small spiral pasta
1 tablespoon olive oil
1 medium brown onion (150g), chopped finely
3 cloves garlic, crushed
300g yellow patty-pan squash, quartered
1 medium red capsicum (200g), sliced thinly
200g sugar snap peas
1 medium carrot (120g), cut into ribbons
1¼ cups (310ml) cream
1 tablespoon wholegrain mustard
2 tablespoons finely chopped fresh flat-leaf parsley

1 Cook pasta in large saucepan of boiling water, uncovered, until just tender; drain.
2 Meanwhile, heat oil in large saucepan; cook onion and garlic, stirring, until onion softens. Add squash; cook, stirring, until just tender. Add capsicum, peas and carrot; cook, stirring, until capsicum is just tender.
3 Place pasta in pan with vegetables, add combined remaining ingredients; stir over low heat until just hot.

on the table in 30 minutes
serves 4 **per serving** 39.6g total fat (23.0g saturated fat); 3122kJ (747 cal); 76.5g carbohydrate; 17.2g protein; 8.3g fibre

Garlic chilli pasta

500g linguine
½ cup (125ml) olive oil
4 cloves garlic, crushed
2 fresh long red chillies, chopped finely
6 anchovy fillets, drained, chopped coarsely
1 cup coarsely chopped fresh flat-leaf parsley

1 Cook pasta in large saucepan of boiling water, uncovered, until just tender; drain.
2 Meanwhile, heat oil in medium frying pan; cook garlic, chilli and anchovies, stirring, about 3 minutes or until garlic and anchovies are soft.
3 Place pasta and anchovy mixture in large serving bowl with parsley; toss gently to combine.

on the table in 20 minutes
serves 4 **per serving** 30.2g total fat (4.4g saturated fat); 2888kJ (691 cal); 85.7g carbohydrate; 16.0g protein; 5.4g fibre

Penne, parmesan and asparagus hollandaise

¼ cup (60ml) white vinegar
1 tablespoon coarsely chopped fresh tarragon leaves
8 whole black peppercorns
4 egg yolks
250g cold unsalted butter, chopped
1 tablespoon lemon juice
375g penne pasta
1kg asparagus, trimmed, chopped coarsely
⅓ cup (25g) grated parmesan cheese

1 Combine vinegar, tarragon and peppercorns in small saucepan; bring to a boil. Reduce heat; simmer, uncovered, until mixture reduces to about 1 tablespoon. Strain vinegar mixture into large heatproof bowl, discard tarragon and peppercorns.
2 Place bowl containing vinegar mixture over large saucepan of simmering water; whisk in egg yolks until mixture is light and fluffy. Gradually add butter, whisking continuously between additions, until hollandaise sauce thickens; stir in juice.
3 Cook pasta in large saucepan of boiling water, uncovered, until just tender; drain.
4 Meanwhile, boil, steam or microwave asparagus until just tender; drain.
5 Place pasta, asparagus, cheese and hollandaise sauce in large bowl; toss gently to combine.

on the table in 35 minutes
serves 4 **per serving** 60.9g total fat (37.4g saturated fat); 3783kJ (905 cal); 66.9g carbohydrate; 20.7g protein; 5.6g fibre
tip be careful not to have heat too high when whisking egg yolks with the vinegar mixture, or you'll end up with scrambled eggs rather than a smooth hollandaise.

Fresh tomato and caper salsa with penne

375g penne pasta
6 medium tomatoes (1.1kg), seeded, chopped finely
⅓ cup (80g) drained capers, chopped coarsely
1 medium red onion (170g), chopped finely
12 basil leaves, torn
12 purple basil leaves, torn
½ cup (80g) toasted pine nuts
balsamic vinaigrette
2 cloves garlic, crushed
⅓ cup (80ml) balsamic vinegar
⅔ cup (160ml) olive oil

1 Cook pasta in large saucepan of boiling water, uncovered, until just tender; drain. Rinse until cold water; drain.
2 Meanwhile, make balsamic vinaigrette.
3 Place pasta in large bowl with remaining ingredients and drizzle with vinaigrette; toss gently to combine.
balsamic vinaigrette place ingredients in screw-top jar; shake well.

on the table in 25 minutes
serves 4 **per serving** 51.7g total fat (6.2g saturated fat); 3453kJ (819 cal); 71.0g carbohydrate; 15.0g protein; 6.6g fibre

Spaghetti with spinach and coppa

⅓ cup (80ml) olive oil
1 clove garlic, crushed
¼ medium red capsicum (50g), chopped finely
½ small brown onion (40g), chopped finely
1 fresh small red thai chilli, sliced thinly
90g coppa (smoked pork), chopped finely
8 spinach leaves, shredded finely
2 tablespoons grated parmesan cheese
375g spaghetti

1 Heat oil in medium frying pan; cook garlic, capsicum, onion, chilli and coppa, stirring, 2 minutes. Add spinach; cook, stirring constantly, 2 minutes. Add cheese.
2 Meanwhile, cook pasta in large saucepan of boiling water, uncovered until just tender; drain.
3 Combine pasta and sauce.

on the table in 35 minutes
serves 4 **per serving** 23.5g total fat (4.6g saturated fat); 2295kJ (549 cal); 65.2g carbohydrate; 17.0g protein; 4.0g fibre

Minestrone on the run

1 tablespoon olive oil
1 medium brown onion (150g), chopped finely
2 cloves garlic, crushed
1 large carrot (180g), chopped coarsely
3 trimmed celery stalks (300g), chopped coarsely
2 medium parsnips (250g), chopped coarsely
2 x 400g cans tomatoes
2 tablespoons tomato paste
3 cups (750ml) vegetable stock
1½ cups (375ml) water
180g small macaroni
400g can borlotti beans, drained, rinsed
¼ cup finely chopped fresh basil
⅓ cup (25g) finely grated pecorino cheese

1 Heat oil in large saucepan; cook onion and garlic, stirring, until onion softens. Add carrot, celery and parsnip; cook, stirring, 5 minutes. Add undrained crushed tomatoes, paste, stock and the water, bring to a boil; cook, uncovered, 5 minutes.
2 Add pasta; boil, uncovered, until pasta is just tender.
3 Add beans; stir over low heat until hot. Stir in basil; serve sprinkled with cheese.

on the table in 35 minutes
serves 4 **per serving** 8.6g total fat (2.2g saturated fat); 1693kJ (405 cal); 57.2g carbohydrate; 17.4g protein; 13.1g fibre
tip use drained canned cannellini beans (or even chickpeas) instead of borlotti beans if you like.

Spinach, bacon and pine nut pasta

4 rashers rindless bacon (250g), sliced thinly
¼ cup (40g) pine nuts
2 cloves garlic, crushed
500g pappardelle pasta
200g baby spinach leaves
⅓ cup (25g) grated parmesan cheese
¼ cup (60ml) olive oil
2 teaspoons lemon juice

1 Cook bacon in small, frying pan; stir until browned lightly. Add pine nuts and garlic; cook, stirring, until browned.
2 Meanwhile, cook pasta in large saucepan of boiling water, uncovered, until just tender. Drain, reserving ¼ cup (60ml) of the cooking liquid. Return pasta to pan.
3 Add bacon mixture to pasta with spinach, cheese, oil, juice and reserved cooking liquid; toss to combine. Serve sprinkled with parmesan cheese flakes, if desired.

on the table in 30 minutes
serves 4 **per serving** 26.3g total fat (4.6g saturated fat); 2943kJ (704 cal); 86.4g carbohydrate; 26.9g protein; 6.2g fibre

Capsicum and pancetta with cellentani

500g cellentani pasta
¼ cup (60ml) olive oil
150g sliced pancetta, chopped coarsely
3 cloves garlic, crushed
3 medium tomatoes (300g), peeled, seeded, chopped
300g roasted red capsicum, sliced thinly
1 cup firmly packed fresh flat-leaf parsley leaves
1 tablespoon baby capers, rinsed, drained

1 Cook pasta in large saucepan of boiling water, uncovered, until just tender; drain.
2 Meanwhile, heat 1 tablespoon of the oil in large frying pan; cook pancetta, stirring, until crisp. Remove from pan.
3 Cook garlic, tomatoes and capsicum in same frying pan; stir until softened. Remove from heat; stir in parsley and capers.
4 Place pasta, tomato mixture and pancetta in large bowl with remaining oil; toss gently to combine.

on the table in 30 minutes
serves 4 **per serving** 20.4g total fat (4.1g saturated fat); 2725kJ (652 cal); 89.7g carbohydrate; 23.2g protein; 6.6g fibre

Tagliatelle with artichokes

500g tagliatelle pasta
1 tablespoon olive oil
1 medium brown onion (150g), chopped coarsely
3 cloves garlic, crushed
3 teaspoons finely grated lemon rind
½ cup (125ml) chicken stock
2 x 400g cans artichoke hearts, drained, sliced thickly
100g butter, chopped
½ cup (40g) finely grated parmesan cheese
2 tablespoons finely shredded fresh mint

1 Cook pasta in large saucepan of boiling water, uncovered, until just tender; drain.
2 Meanwhile, heat oil in large frying pan; cook onion and garlic, stirring, until onion softens. Add rind and stock; bring to a boil. Reduce heat, simmer, uncovered, 1 minute. Add artichoke and butter; stir over medium heat until butter melts.
3 Place pasta and artichoke mixture in large bowl with cheese and half of the mint; toss gently to combine. Serve topped with remaining mint.

on the table in 25 minutes
serves 4 **per serving** 30.3g total fat (16.5g saturated fat); 3085kJ (738 cal); 89.7g carbohydrate; 21.7g protein; 9.1g fibre

Gnocchi with herb and mushroom sauce

Gnocchi are small dumplings made of ingredients such as flour, potatoes, semolina, ricotta cheese or spinach. They make a great base for a full-flavoured sauce such as this – packed with herbs, red wine and mushrooms.

1 tablespoon vegetable oil
1 medium brown onion (150g), chopped coarsely
2 cloves garlic, crushed
400g swiss brown mushrooms, sliced thinly
1 tablespoon plain flour
⅓ cup (80ml) dry red wine
2 teaspoons soy sauce
⅔ cup (160ml) vegetable stock
1 tablespoon sour cream
1 tablespoon coarsely chopped fresh oregano
1 tablespoon finely chopped fresh sage
600g potato gnocchi

1 Heat oil in large frying pan; cook onion, garlic and mushrooms, stirring, until vegetables are just tender. Add flour; cook, stirring, 1 minute.
2 Add wine, sauce, stock and cream to pan; cook, stirring, until sauce thickens slightly. Stir in herbs.
3 Meanwhile, cook gnocchi in large saucepan of boiling water, uncovered, until gnocchi rise to the surface and are just tender; drain.
4 Add gnocchi to herb and mushroom sauce; toss gently to combine.

on the table in 25 minutes
serves 4 **per serving** 8.5g total fat (2.6g saturated fat); 1450kJ (347 cal); 48.6g carbohydrate; 11.6g protein; 6.8g fibre

Fettuccine with cauliflower and broccoli

125g butter
4 cloves garlic, crushed
½ cup (35g) stale breadcrumbs
2 anchovy fillets, chopped coarsely
4 cups (350g) coarsely chopped cauliflower
4 cups (350g) coarsely chopped broccoli
250g fettuccine

1 Heat butter in large frying pan; cook garlic and breadcrumbs, stirring, until breadcrumbs are browned. Stir in anchovy.
2 Meanwhile, bring large saucepan of water to a boil. Add cauliflower and broccoli; cook, stirring to ensure pieces separate. When vegetables are just tender, drain; rinse under cold water, drain.
3 Cook pasta in large saucepan of boiling water, uncovered, until just tender; drain.
4 Place pasta in large bowl with cauliflower, broccoli and breadcrumb mixture; toss gently to combine.

on the table in 30 minutes
serves 4 **per serving** 27.2g total fat (17.1g saturated fat); 2199kJ (526 cal); 51.3g carbohydrate; 15.1g protein; 8.1g fibre

Herbed artichoke and tomato sauce with spirals

2 teaspoons olive oil
1 medium brown onion (150g), chopped finely
2 cloves garlic, crushed
3 x 415g cans crushed tomatoes
1 tablespoon coarsely chopped fresh oregano
1/3 cup coarsely chopped fresh basil
375g large spiral pasta
400g can artichoke hearts, drained, quartered
1/2 cup (40g) finely grated parmesan cheese

1 Heat oil in large saucepan; cook onion and garlic, stirring, until onion softens. Add undrained tomatoes; bring to a boil. Reduce heat, add oregano and basil; simmer, uncovered, about 10 minutes or until sauce reduces by a third.
2 Meanwhile, cook pasta in large saucepan of boiling water, uncovered, until just tender; drain.
3 Place pasta, artichoke and half of the cheese in pan with tomato sauce; toss gently to combine. Serve with remaining cheese.

on the table in 30 minutes
serves 4 **per serving** 7.5g total fat (2.6g saturated fat); 1973kJ (472 cal); 76.6g carbohydrate; 18.8g protein; 9.6g fibre

Ricotta and spinach agnolotti with fennel

20g butter
2 medium fennel bulbs (600g), sliced thinly
2 cloves garlic, chopped finely
300ml thickened cream
625g ricotta and spinach agnolotti pasta
⅓ cup (25g) finely grated parmesan cheese
½ cup loosely packed small mint leaves
⅓ cup (50g) toasted pine nuts, chopped coarsely

1 Melt butter in large frying pan; cook fennel and garlic, stirring, until fennel is tender. Add cream, bring to a boil. Reduce heat, simmer, uncovered, until thickened slightly.
2 Meanwhile, cook pasta in large saucepan of boiling water, uncovered, until just tender; drain.
3 Add pasta to cream mixture with cheese, mint and pine nuts; toss gently to combine.

on the table in 35 minutes
serves 4 **per serving** 53.9g total fat (29.6g saturated fat); 2855kJ (683 cal); 29.1g carbohydrate; 18.9g protein; 6.0g fibre

Fettuccine with green olives and lemon

500g fettuccine
20g butter
4 cloves garlic, crushed
250g small pimiento-stuffed green olives
60g butter, chopped, extra
1 cup (80g) finely grated parmesan cheese
⅓ cup coarsely chopped fresh flat-leaf parsley
2 teaspoons grated lemon rind
2 tablespoons lemon juice

1 Cook pasta in large saucepan of boiling water, uncovered, until just tender. Drain, reserving ½ cup (125ml) of the cooking liquid. Return pasta to pan.
2 Meanwhile, heat butter in small frying pan; cook garlic and olives, stirring, until garlic is soft and olives are heated through.
3 Add olive mixture to pasta with extra butter, cheese, parsley, rind and juice; toss gently to combine. Stir in enough of the reserved cooking liquid to moisten.

on the table in 20 minutes
serves 4 **per serving** 29.6g total fat (15.9g saturated fat); 3035kJ (726 cal); 87.2g carbohydrate; 22.6g protein; 9.8g fibre

Linguine with asparagus and chilli pancetta

500g linguine
150g thinly sliced chilli pancetta, halved
⅓ cup (80ml) olive oil
2 cloves garlic, sliced thinly
250g asparagus, trimmed, sliced thinly
100g baby rocket leaves
¼ cup (60ml) lemon juice

1 Cook pasta in large saucepan of boiling water, uncovered, until just tender; drain. Return pasta to pan.
2 Meanwhile, cook pancetta, in batches, in large frying pan until browned both sides and crisp. Remove from pan and keep warm.
3 Add oil to same pan (there should still be about 1 tablespoon of fat from the pancetta) with garlic and asparagus; cook, stirring, 1 minute or until fragrant.
4 Pour hot asparagus mixture over pasta, add rocket and juice; stir through pancetta.

on the table in 35 minutes
serves 4 **per serving** 25.0g total fat (4.8g saturated fat); 2838kJ (679 cal); 87.1g carbohydrate; 23.1g protein; 5.4g fibre

Salami and vegetable pasta

375g spiral pasta
2 tablespoons olive oil
1 large brown onion (300g), chopped finely
1 large red capsicum (350g), chopped coarsely
3 finger eggplants (180g), sliced thickly
150g sliced salami
400g jar tomato pasta sauce
2 tablespoons chopped fresh flat-leaf parsley
½ cup (40g) parmesan cheese flakes

1 Cook pasta in large saucepan of boiling water, uncovered, until just tender; drain.
2 Meanwhile, heat oil in large frying pan; cook onion, capsicum, eggplant and salami, stirring, until vegetables are tender.
3 Add sauce and parsley to pan; stir until hot.
4 Combine pasta and vegetable mixture; serve topped with cheese flakes.

on the table in 20 minutes
serves 4 **per serving** 28.5g total fat (8.2g saturated fat); 2959kJ (708 cal); 82.0g carbohydrate; 26.6g protein; 7.9g fibre

Fettuccine with char-grilled vegetables

500g fettuccine
2 x 280g jars antipasto char-grilled vegetables
200g baby spinach leaves
1 cup (80g) parmesan cheese flakes

1 Cook pasta in large saucepan of boiling water, uncovered, until just tender; drain.
2 Meanwhile, drain vegetables; reserve ¼ cup (60ml) of oil. Chop vegetables coarsely. Cook vegetables and reserved oil in large saucepan until hot.
3 Toss hot pasta with vegetable mixture, spinach and half of the cheese. Serve, topped with remaining cheese.

on the table in 20 minutes
serves 4 **per serving** 12.4g total fat (4.9g saturated fat); 3206kJ (767 cal); 119.1g carbohydrate; 33.5g protein; 19.5g fibre

Cauliflower chilli spaghetti

¼ cup (60ml) olive oil
700g small cauliflower florets
⅓ cup (50g) pine nuts, chopped
2 cloves garlic, crushed
6 drained anchovies, chopped
½ teaspoon dried chilli flakes
1 tablespoon lemon juice
¼ cup coarsely chopped fresh flat-leaf parsley
375g spaghetti
2 tablespoons olive oil, extra

1 Heat oil in large frying pan; cook cauliflower, stirring, about 10 minutes or until just tender and browned lightly.
2 Add nuts; cook, stirring, until browned lightly. Add garlic, anchovies and chilli to cauliflower mixture; cook, stirring, until mixture is fragrant. Stir in lemon juice and parsley.
3 Meanwhile, cook pasta in large saucepan of boiling water, uncovered, until just tender; drain.
4 Toss cauliflower mixture with spaghetti and extra oil.

on the table in 30 minutes
serves 4 **per serving** 33.2g total fat (4.0g saturated fat); 2746kJ (657 cal); 68.5g carbohydrate; 17.7g protein; 7.3g fibre

Gnocchi with spinach cream sauce

600g gnocchi
30g butter
1 medium brown onion (150g), chopped finely
1 clove garlic, crushed
½ cup (125ml) dry white wine
¾ cup (180ml) cream
¾ cup (180ml) vegetable stock
300g baby spinach leaves, shredded coarsely
½ cup (40g) finely grated parmesan cheese

1 Cook gnocchi in large saucepan of boiling water, uncovered, about
5 minutes or until gnocchi float to the surface; drain.
2 Meanwhile, melt butter in large saucepan; cook onion and garlic,
stirring, until onion softens. Stir in wine, cream and stock; bring to a boil.
Boil, uncovered, 2 minutes.
3 Add spinach and cheese to pan; cook, stirring, until spinach is just
wilted and cheese melts.
4 Serve gnocchi topped with spinach cream sauce.

on the table in 25 minutes
serves 4 **per serving** 30.7g total fat (19.7g saturated fat); 2320kJ
(555 cal); 48.0g carbohydrate; 14.0g protein; 6.1g fibre

Fettuccine with roasted mushrooms and tomato

200g flat mushrooms
200g button mushrooms
200g swiss brown mushrooms
250g cherry tomatoes
½ cup (125ml) vegetable stock
2 teaspoons garlic salt
375g fettuccine
¼ cup torn fresh basil leaves
¼ cup (20g) coarsely grated parmesan cheese

1 Preheat oven to 220°C/200°C fan-forced.
2 Cut flat mushrooms into quarters.
3 Place mushrooms, tomatoes and stock in baking dish; sprinkle with garlic salt. Bake, uncovered, about 20 minutes or until mushrooms are tender and tomatoes softened.
4 Meanwhile, cook pasta in large saucepan of boiling water, uncovered, until just tender; drain.
5 Gently toss mushroom mixture through pasta; sprinkle with basil and cheese.

on the table in 35 minutes
serves 4 **per serving** 3.3g total fat (1.3g saturated fat); 1618kJ (387 cal); 66.0g carbohydrate; 18.5g protein; 7.9g fibre

Vegetable and pasta soup

1 tablespoon olive oil
1 large brown onion (200g), chopped finely
2 trimmed celery stalks (200g), chopped coarsely
2 medium carrots (240g), chopped coarsely
3 cloves garlic, crushed
1 teaspoon dried oregano
¼ teaspoon dried chilli flakes
1 litre (4 cups) boiling water
1 litre (4 cups) vegetable stock
125g tagliatelle pasta
¼ cup coarsely chopped fresh flat-leaf parsley
60g baby spinach leaves, torn

1 Heat oil in large saucepan; cook onion, celery, carrot, garlic, oregano and chilli, stirring, until vegetables are just tender.
2 Add the boiling water and stock to pan; bring to a boil. Add pasta; reduce heat, simmer, uncovered, stirring occasionally, about 15 minutes or until pasta is tender. Stir in parsley.
3 Divide spinach among serving bowls; top with soup.

on the table in 35 minutes
serves 4 **per serving** 6.2g total fat (1.2g saturated fat); 861kJ (206 cal); 29.2g carbohydrate; 8.3g protein; 5g fibre

Ravioli with spinach and sage

500g ricotta and spinach ravioli
300ml cream
¼ cup (20g) finely grated parmesan cheese
100g baby spinach leaves
1 tablespoon small sage leaves
2 tablespoons toasted pine nuts
2 tablespoons parmesan cheese flakes

1 Cook pasta in large saucepan of boiling water, uncovered, until just tender; drain.
2 Meanwhile, place cream and grated cheese in small saucepan; bring to a boil. Reduce heat, simmer, uncovered, 5 minutes or until mixture thickens slightly.
3 Add cream mixture, spinach and sage to ravioli; toss gently to combine.
4 Divide among serving plates, top with pine nuts and cheese flakes.

on the table in 25 minutes
serves 4 **per serving** 49.0g total fat (28.8g saturated fat); 2475kJ (592 cal); 21.4g carbohydrate; 16.1g protein; 3.2g fibre

Russian penne salad

375g penne pasta
2 cups (250g) frozen peas
450g can whole baby beets, drained, chopped coarsely
6 green onions, chopped finely
2 cloves garlic, crushed
2 large dill pickles, chopped finely
¼ cup coarsely chopped fresh flat-leaf parsley
1 cup (240g) sour cream
1 cup (250ml) buttermilk

1 Cook pasta in large saucepan of boiling water, uncovered, until just tender; drain. Rinse under cold water; drain.
2 Meanwhile, boil, steam or microwave peas until just tender; drain.
3 Place pasta and peas in large bowl with beet, onion, garlic, pickle, parsley and combined cream and buttermilk; toss gently to combine.

on the table in 25 minutes
serves 4 **per serving** 26.6g total fat (16.7g saturated fat); 2805kJ (671 cal); 83.1g carbohydrate; 19.7g protein; 9.7g fibre
tip this new take on the classic Russian original is great served with pork loin chops.

Pea and pancetta pasta

375g linguine
50g sliced chilli pancetta, chopped coarsely
2 tablespoons olive oil
2 cloves garlic, crushed
1 cup (160g) shelled fresh peas
150g snow peas, trimmed, sliced thinly
20g butter
½ cup (40g) parmesan cheese flakes

1 Cook pasta in large saucepan of boiling water, uncovered, until just tender; drain.
2 Meanwhile, cook pancetta in large frying pan until browned and crisp. Remove from pan.
3 Heat oil in same frying pan; cook garlic, peas and snow peas, stirring, until just tender. Add pea mixture to pasta with butter; toss well.
4 Serve pasta topped with cheese and pancetta.

on the table in 35 minutes
serves 4 **per serving** 19.5g total fat (6.9g saturated fat); 2299kJ (550 cal); 69.8g carbohydrate; 20.3g protein; 6.5g fibre

Bow ties with zucchini in lemon garlic sauce

375g bow tie pasta
3 medium yellow zucchini (360g)
3 medium green zucchini (360g)
30g butter
1 tablespoon olive oil
2 cloves garlic, crushed
⅓ cup (80ml) vegetable stock
½ cup (125ml) cream
2 teaspoons finely grated lemon rind
⅓ cup coarsely chopped fresh chives

1 Cook pasta in large saucepan of boiling water, uncovered, until just tender; drain.
2 Meanwhile, halve zucchini lengthways; slice halves thinly on the diagonal.
3 Heat butter and oil in large frying pan; cook zucchini and garlic over high heat, stirring, until zucchini is just tender. Add stock; bring to a boil. Reduce heat, add cream, rind and chives; stir until hot.
4 Place pasta in pan with zucchini sauce; toss gently to combine.

on the table in 30 minutes
serves 4 **per serving** 25.9g total fat (13.9g saturated fat); 2408kJ (576 cal); 67.7g carbohydrate; 14.6g protein; 6.4g fibre

Pasta with broccoli and anchovies

375g tagliatelle
600g broccoli, chopped coarsely
½ cup (125ml) olive oil
2 cloves garlic, crushed
4 drained anchovy fillets, chopped
1 teaspoon dried chilli flakes

1 Cook pasta in large saucepan of boiling water, uncovered, until just tender; drain.
2 Meanwhile, cook broccoli in saucepan of boiling water, uncovered, until almost tender; drain well.
3 Heat oil in medium frying pan; cook broccoli, stirring, 2 minutes. Add garlic, anchovy and chilli; cook, stirring, until mixture is fragrant.
4 Combine broccoli mixture with pasta.

on the table in 20 minutes
serves 4 **per serving** 30.0g total fat (4.3g saturated fat); 2546kJ (609 cal); 64.7g carbohydrate; 16.3g protein; 7.5g fibre

Spaghettini with rocket, pine nuts and sun-dried capsicum

500g spaghettini
270g jar sun-dried capsicums
¼ cup (60ml) olive oil
½ cup (80g) pine nuts, chopped coarsely
2 fresh small red thai chillies, chopped finely
2 cloves garlic, crushed
100g rocket, shredded finely
⅓ cup (25g) coarsely grated parmesan cheese

1 Cook pasta in large saucepan of boiling water, uncovered, until just tender; drain.
2 Meanwhile, drain capsicums over small bowl; reserve ¼ cup of the oil. Coarsely chop ½ cup of the capsicum; return remaining capsicum and oil to jar, keep for another use.
3 Heat reserved oil with olive oil in large saucepan; cook pine nuts, chilli and garlic, stirring, until fragrant. Add pasta, chopped capsicum and rocket; toss until rocket is just wilted.
4 Serve pasta sprinkled with cheese.

on the table in 25 minutes
serves 4 **per serving** 33.4g total fat (4.6g saturated fat); 3507kJ (839 cal); 103.1g carbohydrate; 24.9g protein; 12.6g fibre

meat

Grilled lamb and risoni with mustard sauce

450g lamb fillets
500g risoni pasta
1 tablespoon olive oil
2 cloves garlic, crushed
300ml cream
¼ cup (70g) wholegrain mustard
1 cup (125g) frozen peas

1 Cook lamb, in batches, on heated oiled grill plate (or grill or barbecue) until browned and cooked as desired. Cover; stand 5 minutes, slice thickly.
2 Meanwhile, cook pasta in large saucepan of boiling water, uncovered, until just tender; drain.
3 Heat oil in small saucepan; cook garlic, stirring, until fragrant. Add cream and mustard; bring to a boil. Reduce heat, simmer, uncovered, 2 minutes. Add peas; bring to a boil, then remove from heat.
4 Place lamb, pasta and sauce in large bowl; toss gently to combine.

on the table in 35 minutes
serves 4 **per serving** 43.1g total fat (24.2g saturated fat); 3912kJ (936 cal); 90.4g carbohydrate; 43.0g protein; 6.9g fibre
tip risoni is a small rice-shaped pasta that can be served similarly to orzo or rice in salads and soups.

Pork and sage with fettuccine

100g shaved ham
cooking-oil spray
1 tablespoon fresh sage leaves
8 pork leg schnitzels (400g)
250g fettuccine
1 cup (250ml) dry white wine
1 tablespoon brown sugar
150g baby spinach leaves
1 small red onion (100g), sliced thinly
2 tablespoons chopped fresh chives
1 tablespoon olive oil

1 Add ham to large frying pan coated lightly with cooking oil spray; cook, stirring, until browned. Remove from pan; cover to keep warm. Add sage to same pan; cook until just wilted. Remove from pan.
2 Cook pork in pan until browned and just cooked through. Remove from pan; cover to keep warm. Reserve pan for sauce.
3 Meanwhile, cook pasta in large saucepan of boiling water, uncovered, until just tender; drain.
4 Add wine and sugar to same frying pan; boil, uncovered, until reduced by one-third.
5 Place pasta in large bowl with spinach, onion, chives and oil; toss gently to combine. Serve pasta mixture topped with pork, ham and sage; drizzle with wine sauce.

on the table in 30 minutes
serves 4 **per serving** 8.1g total fat (1.6g saturated fat); 1910kJ (457 cal); 47.6g carbohydrate; 35.8g protein; 3.4g fibre

Gremolata lamb salad

250g bow tie pasta
600g asparagus, trimmed, halved crossways
200g green beans, trimmed, halved crossways
1 tablespoon vegetable oil
800g lamb backstraps
2 teaspoons dijon mustard
3 shallots (75g), sliced thinly
⅓ cup (50g) toasted pine nuts
⅓ cup loosely packed fresh flat-leaf parsley leaves
gremolata
2 cloves garlic, chopped finely
1 tablespoon finely grated lemon rind
½ cup finely chopped fresh flat-leaf parsley
lemon dijon dressing
2 tablespoons lemon juice
2 tablespoons olive oil
2 teaspoons dijon mustard

1 Cook pasta in large saucepan of boiling water, uncovered, until just tender; drain. Rinse under cold water; drain.
2 Meanwhile, boil, steam or microwave asparagus and beans, separately, until just tender; drain.
3 Make gremolata.
4 Heat oil in large frying pan; cook lamb, uncovered, until browned and cooked as desired. Spread lamb with mustard; press gremolata firmly onto mustard on lamb. Slice lamb thickly.
5 Make lemon dijon dressing.
6 Place pasta, asparagus, beans and lamb in large bowl with dressing, shallots, pine nuts and parsley; toss gently to combine.
gremolata combine ingredients in small bowl.
lemon dijon dressing place ingredients in screw-top jar; shake well.

on the table in 35 minutes
serves 4 **per serving** 30.7g total fat (5.7g saturated fat); 2955kJ (707 cal); 47.0g carbohydrate; 56.9 protein; 6.8g fibre

Spaghetti and meatballs

500g pork mince
2 tablespoons coarsely chopped fresh flat-leaf parsley
1 clove garlic, crushed
1 egg
1 cup (70g) stale breadcrumbs
1 tablespoon tomato paste
2 tablespoons olive oil
400g can tomatoes
600ml bottled tomato pasta sauce
375g spaghetti
⅓ cup (25g) finely grated romano cheese

1 Combine pork, parsley, garlic, egg, breadcrumbs and paste in large bowl; roll tablespoons of pork mixture into balls. Heat oil in large saucepan; cook meatballs, in batches, until browned all over.
2 Place undrained crushed tomatoes and sauce in same pan; bring to a boil. Return meatballs to pan, reduce heat; simmer, uncovered, about 10 minutes or until meatballs are cooked through.
3 Meanwhile, cook pasta in large saucepan of boiling water, uncovered, until just tender; drain. Divide pasta among serving bowls; top with meatballs, sprinkle with cheese.

on the table in 35 minutes
serves 4 **per serving** 25.4g total fat (6.7g saturated fat); 3444kJ (824 cal); 96.9g carbohydrate; 46.7g protein; 8.9g fibre

Bacon, zucchini and basil pasta

357g penne pasta
1 tablespoon olive oil
4 rashers rindless bacon (250g), sliced thinly
3 medium zucchini (240g), sliced thinly
2 cloves garlic, crushed
2 small tomatoes (160g), seeded, sliced
⅓ cup (90g) crème fraîche
¼ cup small basil leaves
⅓ cup (25g) parmesan cheese flakes

1 Cook pasta in large saucepan of boiling water, uncovered, until just tender; drain.
2 Meanwhile, heat oil in large frying pan; cook bacon and zucchini, stirring, until bacon is crisp and zucchini is browned lightly. Add garlic; cook, stirring, until fragrant.
3 Combine pasta and bacon mixture with tomato and crème fraîche; stir in basil leaves. Serve topped with cheese.

on the table in 30 minutes
serves 4 **per serving** 18.8g total fat (8.7g saturated fat); 2236kJ (535 cal); 66.2g carbohydrate; 22.3g protein; 4.6g fibre

Greek lamb, fetta and eggplant pasta

1 medium eggplant (300g), chopped coarsely
cooking salt
500g lamb fillets
2 tablespoons olive oil
250g large pasta shells
1 medium red onion (170g), sliced
100g baby rocket leaves
2 medium tomatoes (380g), seeded, sliced thinly
¼ cup loosely packed fresh oregano leaves
200g fetta cheese, crumbled
balsamic vinaigrette
¼ cup (60ml) balsamic vinegar
½ cup (125ml) olive oil
2 cloves garlic, crushed
2 tablespoons wholegrain mustard

1 Place eggplant in colander, sprinkle all over with salt; stand 5 minutes. Rinse under cold water; drain on absorbent paper.
2 Meanwhile, cook lamb, in batches, in large frying pan until browned and cooked as desired. Stand 5 minutes; cut into thick slices.
3 Heat oil in same pan; cook eggplant, in batches, until browned all over and tender.
4 Cook pasta in large saucepan of boiling water, uncovered, until just tender; drain.
5 Make balsamic vinaigrette.
6 Place lamb, eggplant and pasta in large bowl with remaining ingredients; drizzle with dressing, toss gently to combine.
balsamic vinaigrette place ingredients in screw-top jar; shake well.

on the table in 35 minutes
serves 4 **per serving** 55.1g total fat (15.1g saturated fat); 3691kJ (883 cal); 48.8g carbohydrate; 46.2g protein; 5.7g fibre

Spaghetti bolognese

1 tablespoon olive oil
1 medium brown onion (150g), chopped coarsely
2 cloves garlic, crushed
2 medium carrots (240g), chopped coarsely
2 trimmed celery stalks (200g), chopped coarsely
500g beef mince
2 x 400g cans crushed tomatoes
½ cup (125ml) dry red wine
⅓ cup (90g) tomato paste
1 teaspoon white sugar
200g button mushrooms, sliced thinly
¼ cup finely chopped fresh basil
375g spaghetti
¼ cup (20g) finely grated parmesan cheese

1 Heat oil in large saucepan; cook onion, garlic, carrot and celery, stirring, until vegetables soften. Add mince; cook, stirring, until mince changes colour. Add undrained tomatoes, wine, paste and sugar; cook, stirring, about 15 minutes or until sauce thickens slightly. Add mushrooms and basil; reduce heat, simmer, uncovered, 10 minutes.
2 Meanwhile, cook pasta in large saucepan of boiling water, uncovered, until just tender; drain.
3 Divide pasta among serving bowls; top with bolognese sauce, sprinkle with cheese. Serve with ciabatta and a green salad tossed with italian dressing, if desired.

on the table in 35 minutes
serves 4 **per serving** 15.4g total fat (5.0g saturated fat); 2834kJ (678 cal); 79.1g carbohydrate; 44.4g protein; 10.7g fibre

Bucatini with moroccan lamb sauce

2 teaspoons olive oil
1 small brown onion (80g), chopped finely
2 cloves garlic, crushed
500g lamb mince
1 teaspoon ground cumin
½ teaspoon ground cayenne pepper
½ teaspoon ground cinnamon
2 tablespoons tomato paste
2 x 400g cans tomatoes
1 large zucchini (150g), chopped coarsely
2 tablespoons finely chopped fresh mint
375g bucatini pasta

1 Heat oil in large saucepan; cook onion and garlic, stirring, until onion softens. Add lamb; cook, stirring, until changed in colour. Add spices; cook, stirring, until fragrant.

2 Stir in paste, undrained crushed tomatoes and zucchini; bring to a boil. Reduce heat, simmer, uncovered, about 15 minutes or until sauce thickens slightly. Stir in mint.

3 Meanwhile, cook pasta in large saucepan of boiling water, uncovered, until just tender; drain. Serve pasta topped with sauce.

on the table in 30 minutes
serves 4 **per serving** 14.9g total fat (5.5g saturated fat); 2521kJ (603 cal); 73.2g carbohydrate; 39.5g protein; 7.2g fibre

Linguine and chorizo in creamy mushroom sauce

300g swiss brown mushrooms, halved
2 tablespoons olive oil
2 cloves garlic, crushed
2 chorizo sausages (400g)
½ cup (125ml) dry white wine
1 cup (250ml) chicken stock
300g sour cream
4 green onions, chopped finely
375g linguine
2 tablespoons finely shredded fresh basil

1 Preheat oven to 240°C/220°C fan-forced.
2 Place mushrooms in large shallow baking dish, drizzle with combined oil and garlic; roast, uncovered, about 15 minutes or until mushrooms are tender.
3 Meanwhile, cook chorizo in heated medium frying pan until browned and cooked through; drain on absorbent paper. Chop coarsely.
4 Place wine in same cleaned pan; bring to a boil. Reduce heat, simmer, uncovered, 5 minutes. Stir in stock and cream; return mixture to a boil. Reduce heat, simmer, uncovered, about 2 minutes or until sauce is hot. Remove sauce from heat; stir in mushrooms and onion.
5 Cook pasta in large saucepan of boiling water, uncovered, until just tender; drain.
6 Place pasta in large bowl with mushroom sauce, chorizo and basil; toss gently to combine.

on the table in 30 minutes
serves 4 **per serving** 70.5g total fat (32.1g saturated fat); 4523kJ (1082 cal); 70.1g carbohydrate; 35.4g protein; 5.9g fibre
tip sprinkle finely grated parmesan cheese and coarsely ground black pepper over individual servings, if you like.

Fettuccine with ham, spinach and asparagus

375g fettuccine
40g butter
250g leg ham, sliced thinly
200g asparagus, trimmed, chopped coarsely
1 teaspoon cracked black pepper
1 clove garlic, crushed
20g butter, chopped, extra
180g baby spinach leaves
½ cup (40g) parmesan cheese flakes
lemon wedges, for serving

1 Cook pasta in a large saucepan of boiling water, uncovered, until just tender; drain. Reserve ⅓ cup (80ml) cooking liquid.
2 Heat butter in large frying pan; cook ham, asparagus, pepper and garlic, stirring, until asparagus is just tender.
3 Place pasta and ham mixture in large bowl with extra butter, spinach, half of the cheese and the reserved liquid; toss until spinach is just wilted.
4 Serve pasta topped with remaining cheese and lemon wedges.

on the table in 20 minutes
serves 4 **per serving** 19.0g total fat (11.2g saturated fat); 2320kJ (555 cal); 64.9g carbohydrate; 28.1g protein; 4.9g fibre

Penne with lamb and roasted capsicum

3 large red capsicums (1kg)
500g lamb fillets
2 tablespoons olive oil
2 teaspoons ground cumin
2 x 415g cans tomato puree
½ cup (60g) drained semi-dried tomatoes, chopped coarsely
375g penne pasta
¼ cup finely shredded fresh basil

1 Quarter capsicums, remove seeds and membranes. Place capsicum on oven tray, skin-side up; roast under heated grill or in very hot oven until skin blisters and blackens. Cover capsicum pieces with plastic or paper for 5 minutes; peel away skin, then slice capsicum pieces thinly.
2 Combine lamb, oil and cumin in medium bowl. Cook lamb, in batches, in large heated oiled frying pan (or grill or barbecue) until browned all over and cooked as desired. Stand 5 minutes; cut into thin slices.
3 Heat large frying pan, add puree, tomato and capsicum; bring to a boil. Reduce heat, simmer, uncovered, about 5 minutes or until sauce thickens slightly.
4 Meanwhile, cook pasta in large saucepan of boiling water, uncovered, until just tender; drain.
5 Place pasta in large bowl with lamb, tomato sauce and basil; toss gently to combine.

on the table in 25 minutes
serves 4 **per serving** 15.9g total fat (3.6g saturated fat); 2964kJ (709 cal); 88.4g carbohydrate; 45.9g protein; 11.7g fibre

Pasta with creamy bacon sauce

500g penne pasta
1 tablespoon olive oil
1 large leek (500g), sliced thinly
4 rashers rindless bacon (250g), chopped coarsely
1 clove garlic, crushed
2 large zucchini (300g), sliced
350g button mushrooms, halved
2 tablespoons dijon mustard
1¼ cups (300g) light sour cream
¾ cup (180ml) milk

1 Cook pasta in large saucepan of boiling water, uncovered, until just tender; drain.
2 Meanwhile, heat oil in large frying pan, add leek, bacon and garlic; cook, stirring, until leek is soft and bacon is browned.
3 Add zucchini and mushrooms to pan; cook, stirring, until zucchini is just tender. Stir in mustard, sour cream and milk; cook, stirring, until hot.
4 Toss sauce through pasta before serving.

on the table in 25 minutes
serves 4 **per serving** 28.3g total fat (13.6g saturated fat); 3285kJ (786 cal); 95.8g carbohydrate; 31.3g protein; 10.1g fibre

Creamy pasta with ham and peas

500g tortiglioni pasta
1 tablespoon olive oil
200g sliced leg ham, chopped coarsely
1 medium brown onion (150g), sliced thinly
1 clove garlic, crushed
300ml cream
1 cup (125g) frozen peas
¾ cup (60g) parmesan cheese flakes

1 Cook pasta in large saucepan of boiling water, uncovered, until just tender. Reserve ¼ cup (60ml) of the cooking liquid; drain pasta and return to pan.
2 Heat oil in large frying pan, add ham; cook, stirring, until crisp. Remove from pan. Add onion and garlic to same pan; cook, stirring, until onion is soft.
3 Add cream, peas and reserved cooking liquid to pan; bring to a boil. Reduce heat, simmer, uncovered, until sauce has thickened slightly.
4 Add sauce, ham and half of the cheese to pasta; toss gently to combine. Serve sprinkled with remaining cheese and cracked black pepper, if desired.

on the table in 30 minutes
serves 4 **per serving** 45.2g total fat (26.1g saturated fat); 3833kJ (917 cal); 91.3g carbohydrate; 32.9g protein; 6.6g fibre

Linguine with lamb, asparagus and gremolata

375g linguine
375g lamb fillets
500g asparagus, trimmed, chopped coarsely
gremolata
⅓ cup finely grated lemon rind
4 cloves garlic, crushed
1 cup coarsely chopped fresh flat-leaf parsley
½ cup (125ml) lemon juice
8 green onions, sliced thinly
1 tablespoon olive oil

1 Cook pasta in large saucepan of boiling water, uncovered, until just tender; drain.
2 Meanwhile, cook lamb on heated oiled grill plate (or grill or barbecue) until browned all over and cooked as desired. Cover, stand 5 minutes; cut into thin slices.
3 Boil, steam or microwave asparagus until just tender; drain.
4 Make gremolata.
5 Pour gremolata over pasta. Add lamb and asparagus; toss gently to combine.
gremolata combine ingredients in small bowl.

on the table in 35 minutes
serves 6 **per serving** 6.2g total fat (1.6g saturated fat); 1417kJ (339 cal); 45.1g carbohydrate; 22.8g protein; 4.3g fibre
tips this recipe is good served warm or at room temperature. Assemble the salad just before serving – the pasta will absorb the dressing if not served immediately.

Rigatoni with spicy pork sausages

300g thin spicy pork sausages
375g rigatoni pasta
1 medium brown onion (150g), chopped finely
1 clove garlic, crushed
500g tomato and basil pasta sauce
½ cup (75g) seeded black olives
100g baby rocket leaves
⅓ cup (25g) grated parmesan cheese

1 Cook sausages in large frying pan until browned all over and cooked through. Drain on absorbent paper; slice thickly.
2 Meanwhile, cook pasta in large saucepan of boiling water, uncovered, until just tender; drain. Reserve ½ cup (125ml) of the cooking liquid.
3 Cook onion and garlic in same frying pan until soft. Add pasta sauce, sausages and olives; simmer, uncovered, until hot.
4 Combine pasta, sauce and reserved cooking liquid in pan or warmed serving bowl; toss well. Add rocket; toss gently. Serve topped with cheese.

on the table in 30 minutes
serves 4 **per serving** 21.0g total fat (8.4g saturated fat); 2700kJ
(646 cal); 85.0g carbohydrate; 25.0g protein; 7.5g fibre

Creamy lamb linguine with mint pesto

500g linguine
2 cups firmly packed fresh mint leaves
2 cloves garlic, crushed
⅓ cup (50g) toasted pine nuts
2 tablespoons grated parmesan cheese
⅓ cup (80ml) olive oil
500g lamb fillets, sliced thinly
300ml cream

1 Cook pasta in large saucepan of boiling water, uncovered, until just tender; drain.
2 Meanwhile, process mint, garlic, pine nuts, cheese and ¼ cup (60ml) of the oil until combined.
3 Heat remaining oil in medium frying pan; cook lamb, stirring, in batches, until browned.
4 Place mint pesto and cream in same pan; stir well. Add lamb and pasta; stir until hot.

on the table in 35 minutes
serves 4 **per serving** 56.5g total fat (25.6g saturated fat); 4422kJ (1058 cal); 89.2g carbohydrate; 45.3g protein; 6.8g fibre

Tomato and bacon macaroni cheese

185g small pasta shells
4 rashers rindless bacon (250g), chopped coarsely
80g butter
1 medium brown onion (150g), chopped finely
1 medium green capsicum (200g), chopped finely
1 teaspoon mustard powder
½ teaspoon sweet paprika
¼ cup (35g) plain flour
1 cup (250ml) milk
420g can tomato soup
1½ cups (190g) coarsely grated cheddar cheese
1 teaspoon worcestershire sauce

1 Cook pasta in large saucepan of boiling water, uncovered, until just tender; drain.
2 Meanwhile, cook bacon in heated large saucepan, stirring, until brown all over; drain on absorbent paper.
3 Melt butter in same cleaned saucepan; cook onion and capsicum, stirring, until vegetables soften. Add bacon, mustard and paprika; cook, stirring, 2 minutes. Add flour; cook, stirring, until mixture bubbles and thickens. Gradually stir in milk and soup; cook, stirring, until soup mixture boils and thickens.
4 Preheat grill.
5 Stir pasta, two-thirds of the cheese, and sauce into soup mixture; pour mixture into shallow 1.5-litre (6-cup) rectangular ovenproof dish. Sprinkle with remaining cheese; place under hot grill until cheese melts and top is browned lightly.

on the table in 35 minutes
serves 4 **per serving** 38.6g total fat (24.1g saturated fat); 2859kJ (684 cal); 52.3g carbohydrate; 30.8g protein; 3.0g fibre
tip you can substitute pizza cheese and chopped salami for the cheddar and bacon, if you prefer.

Pasta with the lot

250g curly lasagne
150g spanish salami, sliced thickly
200g swiss brown mushrooms, sliced thickly
1 medium green capsicum (200g), sliced thinly
2 medium tomatoes (380g), seeded, sliced thinly
4 anchovies, drained, chopped coarsely
100g kalamata olives, seeded
½ cup (125ml) vegetable juice
¼ cup (60ml) red wine vinegar
¼ cup (60ml) olive oil
2 cloves garlic, crushed

1 Cook pasta in large saucepan of boiling water, uncovered, until just tender; drain. Rinse under cold water; drain.
2 Place pasta in large bowl with salami, mushrooms, capsicum, tomato, anchovy, olives and combined remaining ingredients; toss gently to combine.

on the table in 25 minutes
serves 4 **per serving** 29.2g total fat (6.8g saturated fat); 2037kJ (552 cal); 50.7g carbohydrate; 19.5g protein; 4.8g fibre
tips we used a hot and spicy Spanish salami in this recipe but you could use milder cabanossi or peperoni, if you prefer. You can also use tomato juice in the dressing, if you like, instead of the vegetable juice.

Pork and veal meatballs with mushroom sauce

500g pork and veal mince
2 cloves garlic, crushed
¼ cup (25g) packaged breadcrumbs
1 egg, beaten lightly
2 tablespoons olive oil
500g button mushrooms, halved if large
2 teaspoons sweet paprika
½ cup (150g) sour cream
½ cup (125ml) chicken stock
2 teaspoons cornflour
375g fettuccine
¼ cup lightly packed flat-leaf parsley leaves

1 Combine mince, garlic, breadcrumbs and egg in a medium bowl. Roll level tablespoons of mixture into balls.
2 Heat half the oil in large frying pan; cook meatballs until browned all over and just cooked through. Remove from pan, cover to keep warm.
3 Heat remaining oil in same pan; cook mushrooms, stirring, until just tender. Add paprika, stir until fragrant. Stir in combined sour cream, stock and cornflour; cook, stirring, until sauce boils and thickens slightly. Return meatballs and any juice to pan, stir until hot.
4 Meanwhile, cook pasta in large saucepan of boiling water, uncovered, until just tender; drain.
5 Serve pasta with meatballs and mushroom sauce; sprinkle with parsley.

on the table in 30 minutes
serves 4 **per serving** 33.1g total fat (13.7g saturated fat); 3265kJ (781 cal); 71.1g carbohydrate; 46.1g protein; 6.9g fibre

Lamb and pasta with walnut coriander pesto

You will need about 2 bunches of fresh coriander for this recipe, including the roots and stems as well as the leaves.

375g bow tie pasta
4 (320g) lamb fillets
1½ cups firmly packed fresh coriander leaves
½ cup (50g) toasted walnuts
½ cup (40g) coarsely grated parmesan cheese
2 cloves garlic, quartered
½ cup (125ml) olive oil
1 tablespoon drained preserved lemons, chopped finely
½ cup (140g) yogurt
2 teaspoons olive oil, extra
2 teaspoons lemon juice

1 Cook pasta in large saucepan of boiling water, uncovered, until just tender; drain. Rinse under cold water; drain.
2 Meanwhile, cook lamb in large oiled frying pan until browned all over and cooked as desired. Stand 5 minutes; cut into thin slices.
3 Reserve 2 tablespoons of the coriander leaves. Blend or process nuts, remaining coriander, cheese, garlic and oil until mixture forms a smooth paste. Combine pesto with pasta in large bowl.
4 Divide pasta among serving plates, top with lamb and lemon; drizzle with combined yogurt, oil and juice, top with reserved coriander leaves.

on the table in 25 minutes
serves 4 **per serving** 47.8g total fat (9.2g saturated fat); 3524kJ (843 cal); 66.3g carbohydrate; 35.4g protein; 4.3g fibre
tip preserved lemons, a prominent ingredient in North African cooking, are salted lemons bottled for several months; the flavour is subtle and perfumed. To use, rinse well, discard flesh, using rind only.

chicken

Chicken and pecan pasta

You will need to buy a barbecued chicken weighing about 900g for this recipe. Discard skin and bones before shredding the chicken meat.

500g bow tie pasta
½ cup (120g) sour cream
½ cup (150g) mayonnaise
1 tablespoon dijon mustard
2 tablespoons warm water
3 cups (480g) shredded cooked chicken
2 trimmed celery stalks (200g), sliced thinly
1 cup (115g) toasted pecans, halved lengthways
1 small red onion (100g), sliced thinly

1 Cook pasta in large saucepan of boiling water, uncovered, until just tender; drain. Rinse under cold water; drain.
2 Place pasta and combined sour cream, mayonnaise, mustard and the water in large bowl. Add remaining ingredients; toss gently to combine.

on the table in 30 minutes
serves 4 **per serving** 54.5g total fat (13.2g saturated fat); 4535kJ (1085 cal); 96.7g carbohydrate; 48.1g protein; 7.9g fibre

Pappardelle chicken and creamy mushroom sauce

You will need to buy a barbecued chicken weighing about 900g for this recipe. Discard skin and bones before shredding the chicken meat.

2 tablespoons olive oil
1 clove garlic, crushed
1 small brown onion (80g), chopped finely
250g swiss brown mushrooms, sliced thinly
¾ cup (180ml) cream
2 teaspoons finely chopped fresh rosemary
20g butter
500g pappardelle pasta
3 cups (480g) shredded cooked chicken
½ cup (60g) coarsely chopped toasted walnuts
¼ cup coarsely chopped fresh flat-leaf parsley
¾ cup (60g) coarsely grated parmesan cheese

1 Heat oil in large frying pan; cook garlic and onion, stirring, until onion softens. Add mushroom; cook, stirring, until just tender.
2 Add cream and rosemary to pan; bring to a boil. Reduce heat, simmer, uncovered, until sauce thickens slightly. Add butter; stir until butter melts.
3 Meanwhile, cook pasta in large saucepan of boiling water, uncovered, until just tender; drain. Return to pan.
4 Add cream sauce, chicken, nuts, parsley and half of the cheese to pasta; toss gently to combine. Serve sprinkled with remaining cheese.

on the table in 30 minutes
serves 4 **per serving** 55.7g total fat (21.5g saturated fat); 4548kJ (1088 cal); 91.5g carbohydrate; 54.9g protein; 9.3g fibre

Chicken, hazelnut and rocket salad

250g linguine
340g chicken breast fillets
½ cup (75g) toasted hazelnuts, chopped coarsely
100g curly endive
150g baby rocket leaves
⅓ cup (80ml) lime juice
⅓ cup (80ml) olive oil
2 cloves garlic, crushed
2 teaspoons dijon mustard

1 Cook pasta in large saucepan of boiling water, uncovered, until just tender; drain. Rinse pasta under cold water; drain.
2 Cook chicken on heated oiled grill plate (or grill or barbecue) until browned all over and cooked through. Stand 5 minutes; cut into thin slices.
3 Place pasta and chicken in large bowl with hazelnuts, endive, rocket and combined remaining ingredients; toss gently to combine.

on the table in 20 minutes
serves 4 **per serving** 32.8g total fat (3.7g saturated fat); 2541kJ (608 cal); 45.0g carbohydrate; 30.7g protein; 5.5g fibre

Tagliatelle, chicken and peas in mustard cream sauce

You will need to buy a barbecued chicken weighing about 900g for this recipe. Discard skin and bones before shredding the chicken meat.

250g tagliatelle pasta
1 tablespoon olive oil
1 medium brown onion (150g), chopped finely
2 cloves garlic, crushed
½ cup (125ml) dry white wine
1 tablespoon dijon mustard
1 cup (250ml) cream
2 cups (250g) frozen peas, thawed
3 cups (480g) shredded cooked chicken
¼ cup finely chopped fresh garlic chives

1 Cook pasta in large saucepan of boiling water, uncovered, until just tender; drain.
2 Meanwhile, heat oil in large saucepan; cook onion and garlic, stirring, until onion softens. Add wine and mustard; bring to a boil. Reduce heat, simmer, uncovered, 5 minutes.
3 Stir in cream; return mixture to a boil, then simmer again, uncovered, about 5 minutes or until sauce thickens slightly. Stir in drained peas and chicken; stir over low heat until mixture is hot.
4 Place pasta and chives in pan with chicken and pea sauce; toss gently to combine. Serve sprinkled with grated parmesan cheese, if desired.

on the table in 30 minutes
serves 4 **per serving** 38.3g total fat (20.2g saturated fat); 2959kJ (708 cal); 50.5g carbohydrate; 32.4g protein; 6.6g fibre

Creamy chicken and broccoli pasta

250g orecchiette pasta
2 teaspoons olive oil
1 medium brown onion (150g), chopped finely
1 clove garlic, crushed
2 chicken breast fillets (340g), sliced thinly
½ cup (125ml) chicken stock
½ cup (125ml) thickened cream
250g broccoli, chopped finely
1 tablespoon wholegrain mustard

1 Cook pasta in large saucepan of boiling water, uncovered, until just tender; drain.
2 Meanwhile, heat oil in medium frying pan; cook onion and garlic, stirring, until onion is soft. Add chicken; cook, stirring, until chicken is just cooked through.
3 Add stock, cream and broccoli; simmer, uncovered, until broccoli is just tender. Stir in mustard.
4 Place pasta and chicken mixture in large bowl; toss gently to combine.

on the table in 30 minutes
serves 4 **per serving** 16.9g total fat (8.7g saturated fat); 1956kJ (468 cal); 46.4g carbohydrate; 29.9g protein; 4.5g fibre

Chicken liver sauce with curly lasagne

500g chicken livers
½ cup (50g) packaged breadcrumbs
¼ cup (60ml) olive oil
1 medium brown onion (150g), chopped coarsely
4 medium tomatoes (520g), chopped coarsely
½ cup (125ml) chicken stock
¼ cup (60ml) balsamic vinegar
¼ cup (60ml) dry red wine
2 tablespoons coarsely chopped fresh rosemary
375g curly lasagne

1 Halve each trimmed chicken liver lobe; toss in breadcrumbs, shaking off excess. Heat half of the oil in large frying pan; cook liver over high heat, in batches, until browned and cooked as desired.
2 Heat remaining oil in same pan; cook onion, stirring, until soft. Add tomato; cook, stirring, until tomato is pulpy. Add stock, vinegar, wine and rosemary to pan; cook, stirring, until sauce thickens slightly.
3 Meanwhile, cook pasta in large saucepan of boiling water, uncovered, until just tender; drain.
4 Stir pasta and liver into tomato sauce; toss gently to combine.

on the table in 30 minutes
serves 4 **per serving** 20.3g total fat (3.9g saturated fat); 2788kJ (667 cal); 78.2g carbohydrate; 36.9g protein; 5.7g fibre
tip this is our variation of the classic Italian sauce called fegatini di pollo, and is one for those of you who adore the sweet tenderness of chicken livers. Be sure not to overcook them or they will be dry and unappealing.

Creamy pesto chicken with gnocchi

900g chicken thigh fillets
1 tablespoon olive oil
2 cloves garlic, crushed
2 shallots (50g), chopped finely
100g fresh shiitake mushrooms, sliced thickly
½ cup (125ml) dry white wine
¼ cup (70g) sun-dried tomato pesto
300ml light cream
⅓ cup coarsely chopped fresh basil
625g gnocchi

1 Cut each chicken fillet into thirds. Heat oil in large frying pan; cook chicken, in batches, until cooked through. Cover to keep warm.
2 Add garlic, shallot and mushrooms to same pan; cook, stirring, 2 minutes. Stir in wine; simmer, uncovered, until liquid is almost evaporated. Stir in pesto and cream; bring to a boil. Remove from heat; stir in basil.
3 Meanwhile, cook gnocchi in large saucepan of boiling water, uncovered, until gnocchi are just tender and float to the surface; drain.
4 Divide gnocchi and chicken among serving plates; drizzle with creamy pesto.

on the table in 35 minutes
serves 4 **per serving** 49.2g total fat (20.9g saturated fat); 3678kJ (880 cal); 52.1g carbohydrate; 52.9g protein; 5g fibre

Chicken and pea risoni

400g chicken breast fillets
1 litre (4 cups) chicken stock
300g sugar snap peas, trimmed
1 cup (160g) frozen peas
1 tablespoon olive oil
1 small leek (200g), sliced thinly
1 clove garlic, crushed
500g risoni pasta
½ cup (125ml) dry white wine
1 tablespoon white wine vinegar
1 tablespoon finely chopped fresh tarragon

1 Place chicken and stock in medium frying pan; bring to a boil. Reduce heat, simmer, uncovered, 10 minutes or until cooked through. Remove chicken from pan; reserve stock. Slice chicken thinly.
2 Boil, steam or microwave peas, separately, until just tender; drain.
3 Heat oil in large saucepan; cook leek and garlic, stirring, until leek softens. Add risoni; stir to coat in leek mixture. Add wine; stir until wine is almost absorbed. Add reserved stock; bring to a boil. Reduce heat, simmer, uncovered, stirring occasionally, until stock is absorbed and risoni is just tender. Stir in vinegar; remove from heat. Gently stir in chicken, peas and tarragon.

on the table in 35 minutes
serves 4 **per serving** 9.6g total fat (2g saturated fat); 2801kJ (670 cal); 97.1g carbohydrate; 42.5g protein; 7.6g fibre

Bow ties with tenderloins, ricotta, spinach and tomato

375g bow tie pasta
1 tablespoon olive oil
1 medium brown onion (150g), chopped finely
1 clove garlic, crushed
600g chicken tenderloins, chopped coarsely
150g baby spinach leaves
1 cup (200g) ricotta cheese
1 egg
2 teaspoons finely grated lemon rind
2 tablespoons lemon juice
200g grape tomatoes, halved
¼ cup (20g) finely grated parmesan cheese

1 Cook pasta in large saucepan of boiling water, uncovered, until just tender; drain.
2 Meanwhile, heat oil in large deep frying pan; cook onion and garlic, stirring, until onion softens. Add chicken; cook, stirring, over medium heat, about 5 minutes or until cooked through.
3 Place pasta and chicken mixture in large serving bowl with spinach, combined ricotta and egg, rind, juice and tomato; toss gently to combine.
4 Serve sprinkled with parmesan.

on the table in 25 minutes
serves 4 **per serving** 20.7g total fat (7.7g saturated fat); 2851kJ (682 cal); 67.7g carbohydrate; 52.2g protein; 5.6g fibre

Chicken penne with mushroom sauce

375g penne pasta
2 teaspoons olive oil
750g chicken breast fillets, chopped coarsely
250g button mushrooms, sliced thinly
½ cup (125ml) dry white wine
⅓ cup (80ml) tomato juice
3 green onions, sliced thickly
2 small egg tomatoes (120g), seeded, sliced thinly

1 Cook pasta in large saucepan of boiling water, uncovered, until just tender; drain.
2 Meanwhile, heat oil in large frying pan; cook chicken, in batches, until chicken is browned all over.
3 Cook mushrooms in same pan; stirring, until tender. Add wine; bring to a boil. Reduce heat, simmer, uncovered, 2 minutes. Return chicken to pan with juice, onion and tomato; simmer, uncovered, until sauce thickens slightly and chicken is cooked through.
4 Serve pasta topped with chicken and mushroom sauce.

on the table in 30 minutes
serves 4 **per serving** 7.8g total fat (1.6g saturated fat); 2475kJ (592 cal); 65.7g carbohydrate; 55.6g protein; 5.1g fibre

Fettuccine boscaiola with chicken

500g fettuccine
1 tablespoon olive oil
1 medium brown onion (120g), chopped finely
2 rashers rindless bacon (140g), chopped finely
200g button mushrooms, sliced thinly
¼ cup (60ml) dry white wine
⅔ cup (160ml) cream
1 cup (250ml) milk
1 cup (170g) thinly sliced cooked chicken
¼ cup (20g) finely grated parmesan cheese
2 tablespoons coarsely chopped fresh flat-leaf parsley

1 Cook pasta in large saucepan of boiling water, uncovered, until just tender; drain, reserving ½ cup of cooking liquid.
2 Meanwhile, heat oil in large saucepan; cook onion, stirring, until soft. Add bacon and mushrooms; cook, stirring, 1 minute.
3 Add wine, cream and milk to pan; bring to a boil. Reduce heat, simmer, stirring, 5 minutes. Add chicken; stir until combined.
4 Add pasta to pan with cheese, parsley and reserved cooking liquid; toss gently over low heat until hot. Serve sprinkled with freshly ground black pepper, if desired.

on the table in 20 minutes
serves 4 **per serving** 31.5g total fat (16.2g saturated fat); 3411kJ (816 cal); 91.7g carbohydrate; 35.6g protein; 6.0g fibre

Angel hair pasta, chicken and rocket

250g angel hair pasta
1 tablespoon olive oil
1 medium brown onion (150g), chopped finely
750g chicken mince
1 tablespoon tomato paste
700g bottled tomato pasta sauce
2 teaspoons dried basil
80g rocket
2 tablespoons finely grated parmesan cheese
250g coarsely grated mozzarella cheese

1 Cook pasta in large saucepan of boiling water, uncovered, until just tender; drain.
2 Meanwhile, heat oil in large saucepan; cook onion, stirring, until just softened. Add chicken; cook, stirring, 4 minutes. Add paste; cook, stirring, until chicken is cooked through. Add sauce; cook, stirring, 5 minutes. Remove from heat; stir in basil.
3 Preheat grill. Place half of the pasta in oiled 2-litre (8-cup) ovenproof dish. Top with half of the chicken mixture, rocket and parmesan; repeat with remaining pasta and chicken mixture. Top with mozzarella; place under grill about 2 minutes or until mozzarella melts.

on the table in 30 minutes
serves 4 **per serving** 29.4g total fat (12.7g saturated fat); 3327kJ (796 cal); 62.2g carbohydrate; 67.0g protein; 6.2g fibre

Baked pasta and chicken carbonara

You will need to buy a large barbecued chicken weighing about 900g for this recipe. Discard skin and bones befores shredding the chicken meat.

250g spaghetti
1 tablespoon olive oil
2 cloves garlic, crushed
500g button mushrooms, quartered
1 teaspoon coarsely chopped fresh thyme
¼ cup (60ml) dry white wine
¾ cup (180ml) chicken stock
425g jar carbonara sauce
3 green onions, sliced thickly
3 cups (480g) shredded cooked chicken
⅔ cup (50g) finely grated parmesan cheese
⅓ cup (25g) stale breadcrumbs

1 Cook pasta in large saucepan of boiling water, uncovered, until just tender; drain. Rinse under cold running water; drain.
2 Meanwhile, preheat oven to 240°C/220°C fan-forced.
3 Heat oil in large frying pan; cook garlic, mushrooms and thyme, stirring, until mushrooms are browned. Add wine and stock; bring to a boil. Cook, stirring, about 5 minutes or until liquid is reduced by half; remove from heat.
4 Add pasta to mushroom mixture with sauce, onion, chicken and half of the cheese.
5 Combine remaining cheese and breadcrumbs in small bowl. Pour pasta mixture into lightly greased 3-litre (12-cup) baking dish; sprinkle top with breadcrumb mixture. Bake, uncovered, about 10 minutes or until top is lightly browned.

on the table in 35 minutes
serves 4 **per serving** 19.1g total fat (6.2g saturated fat); 2529kJ (605 cal); 53.8g carbohydrate; 48.5g protein; 6.3g fibre

Chicken and fennel spirals

2 medium fennel bulbs (1kg), trimmed, sliced thinly
3 cloves garlic, sliced thinly
¼ cup (60ml) dry sherry
1½ cups (375ml) chicken stock
375g large spiral pasta
2 cups (320g) shredded cooked chicken
200g snow peas, trimmed, sliced thinly
1 cup (240g) sour cream
1 tablespoon coarsely chopped fresh tarragon

1 Preheat oven to 240°C/220°C fan-forced.
2 Combine fennel, garlic, sherry and ½ cup of the stock in large baking dish; roast, uncovered, about 15 minutes or until fennel is just tender.
3 Meanwhile, cook pasta in large saucepan of boiling water, uncovered, until just tender; drain.
4 Return pasta to same cleaned pan with fennel mixture and remaining ingredients; stir over low heat until hot.

on the table in 30 minutes
serves 4 **per serving** 31.5g total fat (17.8g saturated fat); 3160kJ (756 cal); 73.4g carbohydrate; 36.7g protein; 8.5g fibre

seafood

Mediterranean-style mussels with linguine

1kg large black mussels
2 tablespoons olive oil
1 small brown onion (80g), sliced thinly
3 cloves garlic, crushed
2 fresh small red thai chillies, chopped finely
⅓ cup (80ml) dry white wine
2 tablespoons lemon juice
4 medium egg tomatoes (300g), chopped coarsely
375g linguine
½ cup coarsely chopped fresh basil

1 Scrub mussels; remove beards.
2 Heat oil in large saucepan; cook onion, garlic and chilli, stirring, until onion is soft. Add mussels, wine, juice and tomato; bring to a boil. Reduce heat, simmer, covered, stirring occasionally, about 5 minutes or until mussels open (discard any that do not).
3 Meanwhile, cook pasta in large saucepan of boiling water, uncovered, until just tender; drain.
4 Stir pasta into mussel mixture. Remove from heat; stir in basil.

on the table in 35 minutes
serves 4 **per serving** 11.2g total fat (1.7g saturated fat); 2011kJ (481 cal); 70.4g carbohydrate; 18.0g protein; 5.0g fibre
tip we used a pre-packaged combination of plain, spinach- and tomato-flavoured linguine, but you can use any long, narrow pasta you like.

Angel hair seafood laksa

500g uncooked medium prawns
1 tablespoon laksa paste
2 cups (500ml) vegetable stock
2 cups (500ml) water
400ml coconut cream
300g firm white fish fillets, chopped coarsely
250g angel hair pasta
300g baby buk choy, chopped coarsely
4 green onions, sliced thinly
¼ cup loosely packed fresh coriander leaves

1 Shell and devein prawns, leaving tails intact.
2 Cook laksa paste in heated large saucepan, stirring, until fragrant.
Stir in prawns, stock, the water, coconut cream and fish; bring to a boil.
Reduce heat, simmer, uncovered, until prawns change colour and fish
is just cooked.
3 Meanwhile, cook pasta in large saucepan of boiling water, uncovered,
until just tender; drain.
4 While pasta is cooking, stir buk choy, onion and coriander into laksa
mixture; cook, uncovered, until buk choy is just wilted.
5 Divide pasta among serving bowls; top with laksa mixture.

on the table in 25 minutes
serves 4 **per serving** 25.9g total fat (19.3g saturated fat); 2508kJ
(600 cal); 48.9g carbohydrate; 39.8g protein; 5.6g fibre
tips we used ling fillets in this recipe but you can use any firm white fish
fillet you like. You could also increase the amount of prawns called for
and not use any fish. Make this recipe just before serving.

Fettuccine alle vongole

2 tablespoons olive oil
3 cloves garlic, crushed
1 fresh long red chilli, chopped finely
1 tablespoon drained baby capers, rinsed
¾ cup (180ml) dry white wine
¾ cup (180ml) fish stock
2 tablespoons lemon juice
1kg clams
375g fettuccine
½ cup coarsely chopped fresh flat-leaf parsley
¼ cup coarsely chopped fresh chives

1 Heat oil in large saucepan; cook garlic and chilli, stirring, 1 minute. Add capers, wine, stock and juice; bring to a boil. Add clams; cook, covered, about 5 minutes or until clams open (discard any that do not).
2 Meanwhile, cook pasta in large saucepan of boiling water, uncovered, until just tender; drain.
3 Add pasta to clam mixture; toss gently to combine.

on the table in 30 minutes
serves 4 **per serving** 10.5g total fat (1.6g saturated fat); 2002kJ (479 cal); 65.9g carbohydrate; 20.2g protein; 4.0g fibre

Spaghetti marinara

1 tablespoon olive oil
1 medium brown onion (150g), chopped finely
⅓ cup (80ml) dry white wine
⅓ cup (95g) tomato paste
850g canned tomatoes
750g seafood marinara mix
¼ cup coarsely chopped fresh flat-leaf parsley
375g spaghetti

1 Heat oil in large frying pan; cook onion, stirring, until soft.
2 Add wine, paste and undrained crushed tomatoes to pan; bring to a boil. Reduce heat, simmer, uncovered, 10 minutes or until sauce thickens slightly.
3 Add marinara mix; cook, stirring occasionally, about 5 minutes or until seafood is cooked through. Stir in parsley.
4 Meanwhile, cook pasta in large saucepan of boiling water, uncovered, until just tender; drain.
5 Serve marinara over pasta.

on the table in 20 minutes
serves 4 **per serving** 9.1g total fat (1.8g saturated fat); 2704kJ (647 cal); 84.1g carbohydrate; 48.8g protein; 7.5g fibre

Creamy seafood sauce

500g uncooked medium prawns
125g scallops
60g butter
2 cloves garlic, crushed
½ cup (125ml) dry white wine
300ml cream
1 tablespoon cornflour
¼ cup (60ml) water
1 teaspoon lemon juice
1 tablespoon finely chopped fresh flat-leaf parsley
3 green onions, chopped finely
375g fettuccine

1 Shell and devein prawns; chop coarsely. Clean scallops, separating coral; cut scallops in half.
2 Melt butter in large frying pan; cook garlic 1 minute. Add wine; boil 1 minute. Pour in cream; boil 4 minutes.
3 Add blended cornflour and water to cream mixture, stirring, until mixture boils and thickens; add juice. Add seafood to sauce; cook 2 minutes. Stir in parsley and onion.
4 Meanwhile, cook pasta in large saucepan of boiling water, uncovered, until just tender; drain.
5 Combine seafood sauce and pasta.

on the table in 35 minutes
serves 4 **per serving** 46.4g total fat (29.9g saturated fat); 3494kJ (836 cal); 69.3g carbohydrate; 28.8g protein; 3.6g fibre

Tuna and artichoke pasta

500g penne pasta
1 medium lemon (140g)
¼ cup (60ml) olive oil
4 medium tomatoes (760g), chopped
2 cloves garlic, crushed
425g can tuna in oil, undrained, flaked
2 x 280g jars marinated artichoke hearts, drained
½ cup chopped fresh flat-leaf parsley

1 Cook pasta in large saucepan of boiling water, uncovered, until just tender; drain.
2 Meanwhile, peel rind thinly from lemon, avoiding any white pith. Cut rind into thin strips; reserve. Squeeze juice from lemon – you will need 2 tablespoons of juice.
3 Heat 1 tablespoon of the oil in large frying pan; cook tomato and garlic, stirring, until tomato has softened. Add tuna, juice, artichokes and remaining oil and stir until heated through. Stir in parsley.
4 Toss pasta with sauce. Divide among serving bowls; sprinkle with reserved rind.

on the table in 30 minutes
serves 4 **per serving** 30.1g total fat (4.5g saturated fat); 3478kJ (832 cal); 90.5g carbohydrate; 44.0g protein; 9.8g fibre

Spaghetti with anchovies and garlic breadcrumbs

500g spaghetti
12 slices white bread
60g butter
2 cloves garlic, crushed
45g drained anchovy fillets, chopped finely
2 teaspoons finely grated lemon rind
2 tablespoons lemon juice
½ cup finely chopped fresh chives
½ cup (125ml) olive oil

1 Cook pasta in large saucepan of boiling water, uncovered, until just tender; drain.
2 Meanwhile, remove and discard crusts from bread; blend or process bread into fine crumbs.
3 Melt butter in medium frying pan; cook garlic and crumbs, stirring, until browned.
4 Place pasta and crumb mixture in large bowl with remaining ingredients; toss gently until combined. Serve with lemon wedges, if desired.

on the table in 30 minutes
serves 4 **per serving** 44.9g total fat (12.9g saturated fat); 4226kJ (1011 cal); 123.6g carbohydrate; 24.3g protein; 7.0g fibre

Smoked salmon lasagne stacks

8 sheets curly lasagne (about 250g)
400g thinly sliced smoked salmon
1 medium avocado (250g), sliced thinly
⅓ cup (80ml) lime juice
½ cup (125ml) peanut oil
1 tablespoon finely chopped fresh dill
2 teaspoons wholegrain mustard
100g baby spinach leaves

1 Cook pasta in large saucepan of boiling water, uncovered, until just tender; drain. Rinse under cold water; drain, then pat completely dry with absorbent paper.
2 Place two sheets of pasta on board; layer half of the salmon evenly onto sheets. Top each layer of salmon with another sheet of pasta, avocado, another sheet of pasta and the remaining salmon. Top each of the stacks with a sheet of pasta. Cut each stack in half; halve each piece diagonally. Place two pieces of the stacks on serving plates.
3 Place juice, oil, dill and mustard in small jug; whisk until dressing is blended. Place spinach in medium bowl, pour half of the dressing over leaves; toss gently to combine.
4 Drizzle lasagne stacks with remaining dressing; serve with spinach.

on the table in 25 minutes
serves 4 **per serving** 43.8g total fat (8.3g saturated fat); 2918kJ (698 cal); 43.3g carbohydrate; 31.7g protein; 3.5g fibre

Chilli squid fettuccine

500g fettuccine
½ cup (125ml) olive oil
450g small squid hoods, sliced thinly
2 fresh long red chillies, sliced thinly
2 cloves garlic, crushed
250g rocket leaves, torn
100g fetta cheese, crumbled

1 Cook pasta in large saucepan of boiling water, uncovered, until just tender; drain.
2 Meanwhile, heat 1 tablespoon of the oil in large frying pan; cook squid, in batches, over high heat, until tender and browned lightly.
3 Add remaining oil to pan; cook chilli and garlic, stirring, until fragrant. Add rocket; cook, stirring, until just wilted.
4 Place pasta in large bowl with squid, rocket mixture and cheese; toss gently to combine.

on the table in 20 minutes
serves 4 **per serving** 37.5g total fat (8.5g saturated fat); 3566kJ (853 cal); 86.9g carbohydrate; 39.0g protein; 5.4g fibre

Pasta with tuna and pimientos

300g pasta shells
2 tablespoons olive oil
1 medium brown onion (150g), chopped finely
4 cloves garlic, crushed
410g can red pimientos, drained, sliced thinly
425g can tuna, drained, flaked
1 cup (250ml) water
¼ cup (60ml) lemon juice
¼ cup loosely packed fresh basil leaves, torn

1 Cook pasta in large saucepan of boiling water, uncovered, until just tender; drain.
2 Meanwhile, heat oil in large frying pan; cook onion and garlic, stirring, until onion is soft.
3 Stir in pimiento, tuna, the water and juice; bring to a boil. Remove from heat; stir in basil.
4 Top pasta with sauce.

on the table in 20 minutes
serves 4 **per serving** 12.5g total fat (2.3g saturated fat); 2006kJ (480 cal); 57.0g carbohydrate; 31.9g protein; 4.5g fibre

Smoked salmon and dill salad

250g bucatini pasta
2 small fennel bulbs (400g), trimmed, sliced thinly
1 medium red onion (170g), sliced thinly
200g smoked salmon, sliced thickly
¼ cup drained capers, chopped coarsely
½ cup loosely packed fresh dill
½ cup (125ml) crème fraîche
2 teaspoons finely grated lemon rind
¼ cup (60ml) lemon juice

1 Cook pasta in large saucepan of boiling water, uncovered, until just tender; drain. Rinse under cold water; drain.
2 Place pasta in large bowl with fennel, onion, salmon, capers, dill and combined remaining ingredients; toss gently to combine.

on the table in 25 minutes
serves 4 **per serving** 15.7g total fat (8.8g saturated fat); 1797kJ (430 cal); 49.1g carbohydrate; 20.5g protein; 4.5g fibre

Chilli tuna and lemon linguine

375g linguine
2 x 95g cans tuna in oil with chilli
2 teaspoons finely grated lemon rind
1 tablespoon lemon juice, approximately
¼ cup chopped fresh flat-leaf parsley
2 cloves garlic, crushed
¼ cup (60ml) olive oil

1 Cook pasta in large saucepan of boiling water, uncovered, until just tender; drain.
2 Place pasta in large bowl with undrained tuna and remaining ingredients; toss gently to combine.

on the table in 20 minutes
serves 4 **per serving** 25.8g total fat (3.8g saturated fat); 2420kJ (579 cal); 64.3g carbohydrate; 20.6g protein; 3.6g fibre

Penne with tomato salsa and tuna

375g penne pasta
3 medium tomatoes (570g), chopped finely
1 medium red onion (170g), chopped finely
2 cloves garlic, crushed
¼ cup firmly packed, torn fresh basil leaves
425g can tuna in brine, drained, flaked
¼ cup (60ml) balsamic vinegar

1 Cook pasta in large saucepan of boiling water, uncovered, until just tender; drain.
2 Place pasta in large bowl with remaining ingredients; toss gently to combine.

on the table in 35 minutes
serves 4 **per serving** 3.4g total fat (1.1g saturated fat); 1873kJ (448 cal); 67.5g carbohydrate; 33.1g protein; 4.7g fibre

Pasta with smoked salmon

500g spiral pasta
1 cup (250ml) fish stock
300ml cream
200g smoked salmon off-cuts or strips, chopped coarsely
4 green onions, sliced thinly
2 tablespoons finely chopped fresh dill
1 teaspoon finely grated lemon rind
2 tablespoons lemon juice, optional

1 Cook pasta in large saucepan of boiling water, uncovered, until just tender; drain.
2 Meanwhile, place stock and cream in medium saucepan; bring to a boil. Reduce heat, simmer, uncovered, about 5 minutes or until thickened slightly.
3 Place pasta and cream mixture in large bowl with salmon, onion, dill and rind. Add juice; toss gently to combine.

on the table in 20 minutes
serves 4 **per serving** 36.6g total fat (22.4g saturated fat); 3332kJ (797 cal); 88.5g carbohydrate; 27.9g protein; 4.4g fibre

Crisp-skinned ocean trout with linguine

375g linguine
¼ cup (60ml) olive oil
¼ cup loosely packed fresh sage leaves
¼ cup (50g) drained capers, rinsed
6 green onions, cut into 5cm lengths
4 ocean trout fillets (880g), skin on
⅓ cup (80ml) lemon juice
1 tablespoon sweet chilli sauce
2 cloves garlic, crushed

1 Cook pasta in large saucepan of boiling water, uncovered, until just tender; drain.
2 Meanwhile, heat oil in large frying pan; cook sage, capers and onion, separately, until crisp.
3 Cook fish, skin-side up, on heated oiled grill plate (or grill or barbecue) until crisp both sides and cooked as desired.
4 Place pasta in large bowl with juice, sauce, garlic and half of the sage, half of the capers and half of the onion; toss gently to combine.
5 Divide pasta mixture among serving plates; top with fish, sprinkle with remaining sage, remaining capers and remaining onion.

on the table in 30 minutes
serves 4 **per serving** 18.3g total fat (3g saturated fat); 2784kJ (666 cal); 70g carbohydrate; 53.3g protein; 5.5g fibre

Pasta with salmon roe and chervil

The pasta can be cooked up to 2 hours ahead; keep at room temperature.
Toss pasta just before serving.

375g angel hair pasta
2 tablespoons olive oil
1 teaspoon grated lemon rind
1 tablespoon lemon juice
¼ cup finely chopped fresh chives
¼ cup fresh chervil leaves
50g salmon caviar (roe)

1 Cook pasta in large saucepan of boiling water, uncovered, until almost
tender; drain. Return pasta to pan; add oil and toss gently.
2 Toss pasta with rind and juice, herbs and half the salmon roe.
3 Serve topped with remaining salmon roe.

on the table in 20 minutes
serves 4 **per serving** 11.0g total fat (1.7g saturated fat); 1735kJ
(415 cal); 64.2g carbohydrate; 12.5g protein; 3.2g fibre

Smoked cod with rocket pesto on fettuccine

375g fettuccine
500g smoked cod fillets
rocket pesto
150g baby rocket leaves
2 cloves garlic, crushed
¼ cup (40g) toasted pine nuts
¼ cup (35g) toasted pistachios
2 tablespoons lemon juice
½ cup (40g) coarsely grated parmesan cheese
¾ cup (180ml) olive oil

1 Cook pasta in large saucepan of boiling water, uncovered, until just tender; drain.
2 Meanwhile, cook fish in large frying pan until browned both sides; cool 5 minutes then flake with fork into large bowl.
3 Make rocket pesto.
4 Add pasta to fish with pesto; toss gently to combine.
rocket pesto blend or process ingredients to form a paste.

on the table in 30 minutes
serves 4 **per serving** 58.2g total fat (9.3g saturated fat); 4042kJ (967 cal); 67.0g carbohydrate; 42.0g protein; 5.2g fibre

Chilli prawn linguine

500g linguine
⅓ cup (80ml) olive oil
3 cloves garlic, sliced thinly
2 fresh long red chillies, sliced thinly
⅓ cup coarsely chopped fresh flat-leaf parsley
50g wild rocket leaves
1kg uncooked small prawns

1 Cook pasta in large saucepan of boiling water, uncovered, until just tender; drain. Reserve ½ cup (125ml) of the cooking liquid. Return pasta to pan; cover to keep warm.
2 Meanwhile, peel and devein prawns, leaving tails intact.
3 Heat 1 tablespoon of the oil in large frying pan; cook prawns, in batches, until just changed in colour. Remove from pan; cover to keep warm.
4 Heat remaining oil in same pan; cook garlic and chilli until fragrant.
5 Add prawns, oil mixture, the reserved cooking liquid, parsley and rocket to pasta; toss to combine.

on the table in 25 minutes
serves 4 **per serving** 20.5g total fat (3.0g saturated fat); 2939kJ (703 cal); 85.8g carbohydrate; 40.2g protein; 5.0g fibre

Asparagus and salmon pasta salad

375g pasta shells
400g asparagus, trimmed, cut into 5cm lengths
415g can red salmon, drained, flaked
100g watercress, trimmed
1 small white onion (80g), sliced thinly
1 clove garlic, crushed
2 tablespoons wholegrain mustard
2 tablespoons red wine vinegar
2 tablespoons lemon juice
¼ cup (60ml) olive oil

1 Cook pasta in large saucepan of boiling water, uncovered, until just tender; drain. Rinse under cold water; drain.
2 Meanwhile, boil, steam or microwave asparagus until just tender; drain. Rinse under cold water; drain.
3 Place pasta and asparagus in large bowl with salmon, watercress, onion and combined remaining ingredients; toss gently to combine.

on the table in 30 minutes
serves 4 **per serving** 25.2g total fat (4.9g saturated fat); 2654kJ (635 cal); 66.9g carbohydrate; 32.1g protein; 5.7g fibre

Linguine with crab

300g fresh crab meat
1 clove garlic, crushed
2 fresh small red thai chillies, sliced thinly
½ cup (125ml) dry white wine
1 tablespoon finely grated lemon rind
375g linguine
½ cup coarsely chopped fresh flat-leaf parsley
1 small red onion (100g), sliced thinly
⅓ cup (80ml) peanut oil

1 Cook crab, garlic and chilli in large heated oiled frying pan, stirring, until crab is just cooked.
2 Add wine and rind; bring to a boil. Reduce heat, simmer, uncovered, until wine reduces by half.
3 Meanwhile, cook pasta in large saucepan of boiling water, uncovered, until just tender; drain.
4 Place pasta in large bowl with crab mixture and remaining ingredients; toss gently to combine.

on the table in 25 minutes
serves 4 **per serving** 19.7g total fat (3.6g saturated fat); 2324kJ (556 cal); 66.5g carbohydrate; 20.6g protein; 4.0g fibre

Linguine with prawns, peas, lemon and dill

375g linguine
1kg uncooked large king prawns
2 tablespoons olive oil
2 cloves garlic, crushed
1½ cups (180g) frozen peas
2 teaspoons finely grated lemon rind
6 green onions, sliced thinly
1 tablespoon coarsely chopped fresh dill
¼ cup (60ml) lemon juice

1 Cook pasta in large saucepan of boiling water, uncovered, until just tender; drain. Return to pan.
2 Meanwhile, shell and devein prawns; halve lengthways.
3 Heat half of the oil in large frying pan; cook garlic and prawns, in batches, until prawns are just changed in colour. Cover to keep warm.
4 Place peas in same frying pan; cook, stirring, until heated through. Add rind, onion and dill; cook, stirring, until onion is just tender. Return prawns to pan with juice; stir until heated through.
5 Add prawn mixture and remaining oil to hot pasta; toss gently to combine.

on the table in 30 minutes
serves 4 **per serving** 15.7g total fat (2.3g saturated fat); 2441kJ (584 cal); 69.8g carbohydrate; 39.2g protein; 8g fibre

Scallops with asparagus

375g large spiral pasta
2 teaspoons olive oil
500g asparagus, trimmed, cut into 5cm lengths
400g scallops
1 cup (250ml) dry white wine
300ml cream
2 tablespoons fresh dill
1 tablespoon finely shredded lemon rind
1 tablespoon lemon juice

1 Cook pasta in large saucepan of boiling water, uncovered, until just tender; drain.
2 Meanwhile, heat half of the oil in large frying pan; cook asparagus, in batches, stirring, until just tender.
3 Heat remaining oil in same pan; cook scallops, in batches, until cooked as desired. Remove from pan.
4 Add wine to same pan; boil, uncovered, until reduced by three-quarters. Add cream; reduce heat, simmer, uncovered, until sauce thickens slightly.
5 Add pasta to frying pan with asparagus, scallops and remaining ingredients; toss gently over low heat until hot.

on the table in 25 minutes
serves 4 **per serving** 36.5g total fat (22.1g saturated fat); 3152kJ (754 cal); 68.3g carbohydrate; 25.8g protein; 4.5g fibre

Linguine with tuna, lemon and rocket

500g linguine
425g can tuna in oil
2 tablespoons olive oil
1 clove garlic, crushed
2 medium dried red chillies, sliced thinly
⅓ cup (80ml) lemon juice
100g baby rocket leaves

1 Cook pasta in large saucepan of boiling water, uncovered, until just tender; drain. Return to pan.
2 Meanwhile, drain tuna over small bowl; reserve oil – you will need ⅓ cup (80ml) oil.
3 Heat reserved tuna oil and olive oil gently in large frying pan, add garlic and chilli; cook, stirring, until fragrant.
4 Add tuna to pan, break into chunks with a fork. Remove pan from heat; add juice.
5 Add tuna mixture to pasta with rocket; toss gently to combine.

on the table in 15 minutes
serves 4 **per serving** 35.3g total fat (5.3g saturated fat); 3436kJ (822 cal); 86.4g carbohydrate; 36.9g protein; 4.6g fibre

Sardine and fresh tomato pasta

500g tortiglioni pasta
¼ cup (60ml) olive oil
1 large clove garlic, chopped finely
500g ripe tomatoes, chopped coarsely
2 x 105g cans sardines in oil, drained
½ cup lightly packed fresh basil leaves

1 Cook pasta in large saucepan of boiling water, uncovered, until just
tender. Drain, reserving ¼ cup (60ml) cooking liquid. Return pasta to pan.
2 Meanwhile, warm olive oil in medium frying pan; cook garlic gently until
softened but not brown. Add tomato; cook, stirring gently, until tomato
begins to soften. Add sardines; stir until heated through.
3 Add sardine mixture to pasta with basil leaves and reserved cooking
liquid; toss gently to combine.

on the table in 20 minutes
serves 4 **per serving** 20.8g total fat (4.0g saturated fat); 2700kJ
(646 cal); 87.8g carbohydrate; 23.2g protein; 5.9g fibre

Clear prawn and pasta soup

500g uncooked medium prawns
150g tagliatelle pasta, broken roughly
1.25 litres (5 cups) chicken stock
2 cups (500ml) water
20g piece fresh galangal, chopped finely
4cm piece fresh ginger (20g), chopped finely
4 kaffir lime leaves
½ x 10cm stick (20g) finely chopped fresh lemon grass
⅓ cup (80ml) lemon juice
¼ cup (60ml) fish sauce
1 tablespoon sambal oelek
1 fresh small red thai chilli, sliced thinly
¼ cup coarsely chopped fresh coriander

1 Shell and devein prawns, leaving tails intact.
2 Cook pasta in large saucepan of boiling water, uncovered, until just tender; drain.
3 Meanwhile, combine stock, the water, galangal, ginger, lime leaves and lemon grass in large saucepan; bring to a boil. Boil, uncovered, about 5 minutes or until reduced by a quarter. Add juice, sauce, sambal and prawns, reduce heat; cook, uncovered, until prawns just change in colour. Remove from heat; discard lime leaves. Add chilli and coriander.
4 Divide pasta and prawn mixture among serving bowls; ladle soup over the top.

on the table in 25 minutes
serves 4 **per serving** 2.3g total fat (0.8g saturated fat); 991kJ (237 cal); 30.6g carbohydrate; 22.0g protein; 2.0g fibre

Tuna, olive and rocket pasta

250g angel hair pasta
425g can yellowfin tuna chunks in olive oil, drained, flaked
⅓ cup (55g) seeded kalamata olives, quartered lengthways
250g cherry tomatoes, halved
⅓ cup (50g) toasted pine nuts
100g baby rocket leaves
dressing
2 tablespoons olive oil
1 tablespoon finely grated lemon rind
¼ cup (60ml) lemon juice
1 clove garlic, crushed
1 tablespoon dijon mustard

1 Cook pasta in large saucepan of boiling water, uncovered, until just tender; drain.
2 Place pasta in large bowl with tuna, olives, tomatoes, pine nuts and rocket.
3 Make dressing, drizzle over pasta mixture; toss gently to combine.
dressing place ingredients in screw-top jar; shake well.

on the table in 30 minutes
serves 4 **per serving** 30.9g total fat (3.9g saturated fat); 2533kJ (606 cal); 48.9g carbohydrate; 31.0g protein; 4.6g fibre

Saganaki prawn pasta

375g small spiral pasta
500g uncooked medium prawns
2 teaspoons olive oil
1 small brown onion (100g), chopped finely
2 cloves garlic, crushed
600ml bottled tomato pasta sauce
1 cup (250ml) vegetable stock
200g fetta cheese, crumbled
2 tablespoons coarsely chopped fresh oregano

1 Cook pasta in large saucepan of boiling water, uncovered, until just tender; drain.
2 Meanwhile, shell and devein prawns, leaving tails intact.
3 Heat oil in medium saucepan; cook onion and garlic, stirring, until onion is soft. Add prawns; cook, stirring, until prawns change in colour.
4 Add sauce and stock to pan; bring to a boil. Reduce heat, simmer, uncovered, about 2 minutes or until hot.
5 Place pasta in large bowl with prawn mixture, cheese and oregano; toss gently to combine.

on the table in 25 minutes
serves 4 **per serving** 17.0g total fat (8.5g saturated fat); 2713kJ (649 cal); 83.7g carbohydrate; 36.0g protein; 7.0g fibre

Spaghetti with mussels and clams

500g mussels
500g clams
¼ cup (60ml) water
¼ cup (60ml) dry white wine
500g spaghetti
⅓ cup (80ml) olive oil
2 cloves garlic, crushed
1 fresh small red thai chilli, chopped finely
2 medium tomatoes (380g), seeded, chopped coarsely
½ cup coarsely chopped fresh flat-leaf parsley

1 Scrub mussels; remove beards. Rinse clams.
2 Combine the water and wine in large saucepan; bring to a boil. Add mussels and clams; reduce heat, simmer, covered, about 5 minutes or until mussels open (discard any that do not). Strain cooking liquid through fine sieve into medium bowl; reserve ⅓ cup, discard remainder. Strain reserved cooking liquid again, into small jug. Cover mussels and clams to keep warm.
3 Meanwhile, cook pasta in large saucepan of boiling water, uncovered, until just tender; drain.
4 Heat oil in large frying pan; cook garlic and chilli, stirring, until fragrant. Add tomato and reserved cooking liquid; bring to a boil.
5 Place pasta, mussels, clams and tomato mixture in large bowl with parsley; toss gently to combine.

on the table in 30 minutes
serves 4 **per serving** 20.2g total fat (3.0g saturated fat); 2692kJ (644 cal); 87.7g carbohydrate; 22.0g protein; 5.2g fibre

Linguine with tuna, chilli and fresh tomato

375g linguine
2 x 185g cans tuna in chilli oil
500g ripe tomatoes, chopped coarsely
1 fresh large red chilli, sliced
¼ cup loosely packed fresh oregano leaves
⅓ cup (80ml) lemon juice
¼ cup (60ml) olive oil

1 Cook pasta in large saucepan of boiling water, uncovered, until just tender; drain.
2 Meanwhile, drain tuna, reserving 1 tablespoon of the oil. Place tuna in large bowl; flake with fork.
3 Add pasta to bowl with tomatoes, chilli, oregano, juice, olive oil and reserved chilli oil; toss gently to combine.

on the table in 20 minutes
serves 4 **per serving** 8.9g total fat (1.3g saturated fat); 832kJ (199 cal); 20.0g carbohydrate; 9.1g protein; 1.4g fibre

glossary

almonds flat, pointy-tipped nuts with a pitted brown shell enclosing a creamy white kernel covered by a brown skin.
flaked are paper-thin almond slices.

artichoke hearts tender centre of the globe artichoke; can be harvested from the plant after the prickly choke is removed. Cooked hearts can be bought from delicatessens or canned in brine or oil.

baby beets canned baby beetroot, also called red beets; firm, round root vegetable.

bacon rashers also known as bacon slices; made from cured and smoked pork side.

basil, purple has large purple leaves and sweet, almost gingery flavour.

basil, sweet the most common variety; used extensively in Italian dishes and one of the main ingredients in pesto.

borlotti beans also called roman beans or pink beans, can be eaten fresh or dried. Interchangeable with pinto beans – both are pale pink or beige with dark red streaks.

breadcrumbs fresh usually white bread, processed into crumbs.
packaged prepared fine-textured, crunchy white breadcrumbs.

stale crumbs made by grating or processing 1- or 2-day-old bread.

broad beans also called fava, windsor and horse beans; available dried, fresh, canned and frozen. Fresh should be peeled twice (discarding the outer long green pod and the beige-green tough inner shell); the frozen beans have had their pods removed but the beige shell still needs removal.

buk choy also called bok choy, pak choi, chinese white cabbage or chinese chard; has a fresh, mild mustard taste. Use both stems and leaves, stir-fried or braised. Baby buk choy, also known as pak kat farang or shanghai bok choy, is much smaller and more tender. Its mildly acrid, distinctively appealing taste has made it one of the most common Asian greens.

butter we use salted butter unless stated otherwise; 125g is equal to 1 stick (4 ounces). Unsalted or "sweet" butter has no salt added.

buttermilk is actually low in fat (0.6–2.0 per cent per 100ml). Originally the term given to the slightly sour liquid left after butter was churned from cream; today it is made from no-fat or low-fat

milk to which specific bacterial cultures are added during the manufacturing process. It is readily available from the dairy section in supermarkets. It's a good low-fat substitute for dairy products such as cream or sour cream in some baking and salad dressings.

capers the grey-green buds of a warm climate (usually Mediterranean) shrub, sold either dried and salted or pickled in a vinegar brine; baby capers are also available in brine or dried in salt.

capsicum also called pepper or bell pepper. Discard seeds and membranes before use.

caraway seeds the small, half-moon-shaped dried seed from a member of the parsley family; adds a sharp anise flavour.

cheese
blue mould-treated cheese mottled with blue veining. Varieties include firm and crumbly stilton types and mild, creamy brie-like cheeses.

bocconcini from the diminutive of "boccone", meaning mouthful in Italian; walnut-sized, baby mozzarella, a delicate, semi-soft, white cheese traditionally made from buffalo milk. Sold fresh, it spoils rapidly so will only keep, refrigerated in brine, for 1 or 2 days at the most.

brie soft-ripened cow-milk cheese with a delicate, creamy texture and a rich, sweet taste. Best served at room temperature after a brief period of ageing; should have a bloomy white rind and creamy, voluptuous centre which becomes runny with ripening.

cheddar the most common cow-milk tasty cheese; should be aged, hard and have a pronounced bite. We use a version with no more than 20 per cent fat when calling for low-fat cheese.

cream cheese commonly known as philadelphia or philly; a soft cow-milk cheese.

fetta Greek in origin; a crumbly textured goat- or sheep-milk cheese having a sharp, salty taste. Ripened and stored in salted whey; particularly good cubed and tossed into salads. We use a version having no more than 15 per cent fat when calling for low-fat cheese.

fontina a smooth, firm Italian cow-milk cheese with a creamy, nutty taste and brown or red rind; an ideal melting or grilling cheese.

goat made from goat milk, has an earthy, strong taste. Available in soft, crumbly and firm textures, in various shapes and sizes; often rolled in ash or herbs.

gorgonzola a creamy Italian blue cheese with a mild, sweet taste; good served with fruit or used to flavour sauces (especially pasta).

haloumi a Greek Cypriot cheese with a semi-firm, spongy texture and very salty yet sweet flavour. Ripened and stored in salted whey; it's best grilled or fried, and holds its shape well on being heated. Should be eaten while still warm as it becomes tough and rubbery on cooling.

mascarpone an Italian fresh cultured-cream product made similar to yogurt. Whiteish to creamy yellow in colour, with a buttery-rich, luscious texture. Soft, creamy and spreadable.

mozzarella soft, spun-curd cheese; originating in southern Italy, it was traditionally made from water-buffalo milk. Now generally made from cow milk, it is the most popular pizza cheese because of its low melting point and elasticity when heated. We use a version having no more than 17.5 per

cent fat when calling for a low-fat cheese.

parmesan also called parmigiano, is a hard, grainy cow-milk cheese originating in the Parma region of Italy. The curd is salted in brine for a month before being aged for up to 2 years, preferably in humid conditions.

pecorino Italian generic name for sheep-milk cheeses. This family of hard, white to pale-yellow cheeses, traditionally made in the Italian winter and spring when sheep graze on natural pastures, have been matured for 8 to 12 months. They are classified according to the area in which they were produced — romano from Rome, sardo from Sardinia, siciliano from Sicily and toscano from Tuscany. If you can't find it, use parmesan.

pizza cheese a commercial blend of grated mozzarella, cheddar and parmesan.

ricotta a soft, sweet, moist, white cow-milk cheese with a low fat content (about 8.5 per cent) and a slightly grainy texture. It roughly translates as "cooked again" and refers to ricotta's manufacture from a whey that is itself a by-product of other cheese making.

chervil also called cicily; mildly fennel-flavoured member of the parsley family with curly dark-green leaves. Available fresh and dried but, like all herbs, is best fresh.

chilli always use rubber gloves when handling fresh chillies as they can burn your skin. We use unseeded chillies in our recipes as the seeds contain the heat; use fewer chillies rather than seeding the lot.

dried flakes also sold as crushed chilli; dehydrated deep-red extremely fine slices and whole seeds.

sweet chilli sauce comparatively mild, fairly sticky and runny bottled sauce made from red chillies, sugar, garlic and white vinegar.

thai also called "scuds"; tiny, very hot and bright red in colour.

chives related to the onion and leek; has a subtle onion flavour.

chorizo sausage of Spanish origin, made of coarsely ground pork and highly seasoned with garlic and chilli.

cinnamon available in the piece (called sticks or quills) and a powder; used universally as a sweet, fragrant flavouring in sweet and savoury foods.

clams also known as vongole; we use a small ridge-shelled variety of this bivalve mollusc.

cornflour also called cornstarch. Available made from corn or wheat (wheaten cornflour, gluten-free, gives a lighter texture in cakes).

cornichons French for gherkin, a very small variety of cucumber.

cos lettuce also called romaine lettuce; the traditional caesar salad lettuce. Long, with leaves ranging from dark green to almost white near the core; leaves have a stiff centre rib that gives a slight cupping effect to the leaf on either side.

crème fraîche a mature, naturally fermented cream (minimum fat content 35 per cent) with a velvety texture and slightly tangy, nutty flavour. This French variation of sour cream, can boil without curdling and is used in sweet and savoury dishes.

cumin also called zeera or comino; resembling caraway in size, cumin is the dried seed of a plant related to the parsley family. Available dried as seeds or ground.

dill also called dill weed; used fresh or dried, in seed form or ground. It has an anise/celery sweetness. Distinctive

feathery, frond-like fresh leaves are grassier and more subtle than the seeds or dried version.

eggs some recipes may call for raw or barely cooked eggs; exercise caution if there is a salmonella problem in your area, particularly in food eaten by children and pregnant women.

fennel bulbs also known as finocchio or anise; a crunchy green vegetable slightly resembling celery.

fish sauce called naam pla on the label if Thai-made, nuoc naam if Vietnamese; the two are almost identical. Made from pulverised salted fermented fish (most often anchovies); has a pungent smell and strong taste. Available in varying degrees of intensity, so use according to your taste.

flour, plain also called all-purpose; unbleached wheat flour is the best for baking.

ginger also called green or root ginger; the thick gnarled root of a tropical plant. Can be kept, peeled, covered with dry sherry in a jar and refrigerated, or frozen in an airtight container.

green beans also called french or string beans; when cooked, this long thin bean is eaten entirely.

hazelnuts also called filberts; plump, grape-sized, rich, sweet nut with a brown skin that is removed by rubbing heated nuts together vigorously in a tea-towel.

kaffir lime leaves also called bai magrood, looks like two glossy dark green leaves joined end to end in a rounded hourglass shape. Used fresh or dried in many South-East Asian dishes, they are used like bay leaves or curry leaves, especially in Thai cooking. Sold fresh, dried or frozen, dried leaves are less potent so double the number if using them as a substitute for fresh; a strip of fresh lime peel may be substituted for each kaffir lime leaf.

kumara the Polynesian name of orange-fleshed sweet potato. Bake, boil, mash or fry similarly to other potatoes.

lamb
backstraps also known as eye of loin; the larger fillet from a row of loin chops or cutlets.

fillets fine texture, most expensive and extremely tender.

lebanese cucumber short, slender and thin-skinned. Probably the most popular variety for its tender, edible skin, tiny, yielding seeds, and sweet, fresh taste.

leek a member of the onion family, the leek resembles a green onion but is much larger and more subtle in flavour.

lemon grass also called takrai, serai or serah. A tall, clumping, lemon-smelling and tasting, sharp-edged aromatic tropical grass; the white lower part of the stem is used, finely chopped.

mayonnaise we use whole-egg mayonnaise.

mince meat also called ground meat, as in beef, pork, lamb and veal.

mizuna Japanese in origin; the frizzy green salad leaves have a delicate mustard flavour.

mushroom
button small, cultivated white mushrooms with a mild flavour. When a recipe in this book calls for an unspecified type of mushroom, use button.

flat large and flat with a rich earthy flavour; ideal for filling and barbecuing. Sometimes misnamed field mushrooms which are wild mushrooms.

shiitake, fresh are also called chinese black, forest or golden oak mushrooms. Although cultivated, they have the earthiness and taste of wild mushrooms. Large and meaty.

swiss brown also called roman or cremini.

Light to dark brown mushrooms with full-bodied flavour; suitable for casseroles or being stuffed and baked.

mussels should only be bought from a reliable fish market: they must be tightly closed when bought, indicating they are alive. Before cooking, scrub shells with a strong brush and remove the beards; do not eat any that do not open after cooking. Varieties include black and green-lip.

mustard
dijon also known as french. Pale brown, creamy, distinctively flavoured and fairly mild.

wholegrain made from crushed mustard seeds and dijon-style french mustard.

nutmeg a strong and very pungent spice ground from the dried nut of an evergreen tree native to Indonesia. Usually ground, the flavour is more intense from a whole nut, available from spice shops, so it's best to grate your own.

oil
olive made from ripened olives. Extra virgin and virgin are the first and second press, respectively, of the olives and are considered the best; the "extra light" or "light" on other types refers to taste not fat levels.

peanut pressed from ground peanuts; most commonly used oil in Asian cooking because of its high smoke point (capacity to handle high heat without burning).

sesame made from roasted, crushed, white sesame seeds; used as a flavouring rather than as a cooking medium.

vegetable any of a number of oils sourced from plants rather than animal fats.

onion

green also called scallion or (incorrectly) shallot; an immature onion picked before the bulb has formed, having a long, bright-green edible stalk.

red also called spanish, red spanish or bermuda onion; a sweet-flavoured, large, purple-red onion.

pancetta an Italian unsmoked bacon, pork belly cured in salt and spices then rolled into a sausage shape and dried for several weeks. Hot pancetta is lean pork belly first salted and cured then spiced and rolled into a fat loaf; used in pasta sauces and meat dishes, or eaten on its own.

paprika ground dried sweet red capsicum (bell pepper); varieties available include sweet, hot, mild and smoked.

parsley, flat-leaf also known as continental or italian parsley. An extremely versatile herb with a fresh, slightly earthy flavour.

patty-pan squash also called crookneck or custard marrow pumpkins; a round, slightly flat summer squash, yellow to pale green in colour with a scalloped edge. Harvested young, it has firm white flesh and a distinct flavour.

pecan native to the US and now grown locally; pecans are golden brown, buttery and rich. Used in savoury and sweet dishes; walnuts are a good substitute.

pine nuts also known as pignoli; not in fact a nut but a small, cream-coloured kernel from pine cones. They are best roasted before use to bring out the flavour.

pistachios green, delicately flavoured nuts inside hard off-white shells. Available salted or unsalted in their shells, as well as shelled.

pork, leg schnitzel steak is usually cut from the leg or rump.

prawns also known as shrimp.

prosciutto a kind of unsmoked Italian ham; salted, air-cured and aged, usually eaten uncooked.

rocket also called arugula, rugula and rucola; peppery green leaf eaten raw in salads or used in cooking. Baby rocket leaves are smaller and less peppery.

rosemary pungent herb with long, thin pointy leaves; use large and small sprigs, and finely chopped leaves.

sage pungent herb with narrow, grey-green leaves; slightly bitter with a slightly musty mint aroma. Dried sage comes whole, crumbled or ground.

sambal oelek also ulek or olek; Indonesian in origin, this is a salty paste made from ground chillies and vinegar.

scallops a bivalve mollusc with fluted shell valve; we use scallops with coral (roe) attached.

sesame seeds black and white are the most common variety.

shallots also called french shallots, golden shallots or eschalots. Small, elongated, brown-skinned members of the onion family; they grow in tight clusters like garlic.

snow peas also called mangetout; a variety of garden pea, eaten pod and all. Are available from supermarkets or greengrocers and are usually eaten raw in salads or sandwiches.

soy sauce also known as sieu; made from fermented soybeans. Several varieties are available in supermarkets and Asian food stores; we use Japanese soy sauce unless stated otherwise.

spinach also known as english spinach and incorrectly, silverbeet.

squid hood also called calamari; a type of mollusc. Buy squid hoods to make preparation and cooking faster.

sugar snap peas also called honey snap peas; fresh small pea can be eaten whole, pod and all.

sugar

brown an extremely soft, fine granulated sugar retaining molasses for its characteristic colour and flavour.

white coarse, granulated table sugar, also known as crystal sugar.

tabasco sauce brand-name of an extremely fiery sauce made from vinegar, hot red peppers and salt.

tapenade a thick paste made from black or green olives, anchovies, capers, olive oil and lemon juice.

tarragon often called the king of herbs by the French, it is an essential in many classic sauces.

thyme a member of the mint family. The "household" variety, simply called thyme, is French thyme; it has tiny grey-green leaves that give off a pungent minty, light-lemon aroma.

tomato

canned whole peeled tomatoes in natural juice; available crushed, diced or chopped. Use undrained.

cherry also called tiny tim or tom thumb tomatoes; small and round.

egg also called plum or roma; smallish, oval-shaped tomatoes much used in Italian cooking or salads.

grape small, long oval-shaped tomatoes with a good tomato flavour.

paste triple-concentrated tomato puree used to flavour soups, stews, sauces and casseroles.

puree canned pureed tomatoes (not paste); substitute with fresh peeled and pureed tomatoes.

semi-dried partially dried tomato pieces in olive oil; softer and juicier than sun-dried, they do not keep as long.

sun-dried tomato pieces that have been dried with salt; this dehydrates the tomato and concentrates the flavour. We use sun-dried tomatoes in oil, unless stated otherwise.

vinegar

balsamic originally from Modena, Italy, there are now many on the market ranging in pungency and quality depending on how, and for how long, they have been aged. Quality can be determined up to a point by price; use the most expensive sparingly.

rice a colourless vinegar made from fermented rice; flavoured with sugar and salt. Also called seasoned rice vinegar; sherry can be substituted.

wine (red and white) made from red and white wines, respectively.

walnuts a good source of fibre and healthy oils; also contains a range of vitamins, minerals and other beneficial phytochemicals.

watercress one of a large group of peppery greens used raw in dips, salads and sandwiches, or cooked in soups. Very perishable, use as soon as possible after purchase.

worcestershire sauce thin, dark-brown spicy sauce; used as a seasoning for meat, gravies and cocktails.

yogurt we use plain full-cream yogurt unless stated otherwise. If a recipe in this book calls for low-fat yogurt, we use one with a fat content of less than 0.2 per cent.

zucchini also called courgette; its flowers are edible.

index

conversion chart

MEASURES

One Australian metric measuring cup holds approximately 250ml, one Australian metric tablespoon holds 20ml, one Australian metric teaspoon holds 5ml.

The difference between one country's measuring cups and another's is within a two- or three-teaspoon variance, and will not affect your cooking results.North America, New Zealand and the United Kingdom use a 15ml tablespoon.

All cup and spoon measurements are level. The most accurate way of measuring dry ingredients is to weigh them. When measuring liquids, use a clear glass or plastic jug with the metric markings.

We use large eggs with an average weight of 60g.

LIQUID MEASURES

METRIC	IMPERIAL
30ml	1 fluid oz
60ml	2 fluid oz
100ml	3 fluid oz
125ml	4 fluid oz
150ml	5 fluid oz (¼ pint/1 gill)
190ml	6 fluid oz
250ml	8 fluid oz
300ml	10 fluid oz (½ pint)
500ml	16 fluid oz
600ml	20 fluid oz (1 pint)
1000ml (1 litre)	1¾ pints

LENGTH MEASURES

METRIC	IMPERIAL
3mm	⅛in
6mm	¼in
1cm	½in
2cm	¾in
2.5cm	1in
5cm	2in
6cm	2½in
8cm	3in
10cm	4in
13cm	5in
15cm	6in
18cm	7in
20cm	8in
23cm	9in
25cm	10in
28cm	11in
30cm	12in (1ft)

DRY MEASURES

METRIC	IMPERIAL
15g	½oz
30g	1oz
60g	2oz
90g	3oz
125g	4oz (¼lb)
155g	5oz
185g	6oz
220g	7oz
250g	8oz (½lb)
280g	9oz
315g	10oz
345g	11oz
375g	12oz (¾lb)
410g	13oz
440g	14oz
470g	15oz
500g	16oz (1lb)
750g	24oz (1½lb)
1kg	32oz (2lb)

OVEN TEMPERATURES

These oven temperatures are only a guide for conventional ovens.
For fan-forced ovens, check the manufacturer's manual.

	°C (CELSIUS)	°F (FAHRENHEIT)	GAS MARK
Very slow	120	250	½
Slow	150	275 – 300	1 – 2
Moderately slow	160	325	3
Moderate	180	350 – 375	4 – 5
Moderately hot	200	400	6
Hot	220	425 – 450	7 – 8
Very hot	240	475	9

Editorial director Susan Tomnay
Creative director Hieu Chi Nguyen
Food director Pamela Clark
Food editor Louise Patniotis
Senior editor Stephanie Kistner
Designer Caryl Wiggins
Nutrition information Rebecca Squadrito
Director of sales Brian Cearnes
Marketing manager Bridget Cody
Production manager Cedric Taylor

Chief executive officer Ian Law
Group publisher Pat Ingram
General manager Christine Whiston
Editorial director (WW) Deborah Thomas

WW food team Lyndey Milan, Alexandra Elliott, Frances Abdallaoui

Produced by ACP Books, Sydney.
Printing by Toppan Printing Co., Hong Kong
Published by ACP Magazines Ltd, 54 Park St, Sydney
GPO Box 4088, Sydney, NSW 2001
phone +61 2 9282 8618 fax +61 2 9267 9438
acpbooks@acpmagazines.com.au www.acpbooks.com.au
To order books phone 136 116 (within Australia)
Send recipe enquiries to recipeenquiries@acpmagazines.com.au

RIGHTS ENQUIRIES
Laura Bamford, Director ACP Books
lbamford@acpuk.com

Australia Distributed by Network Services,
phone +61 2 9282 8777 fax +61 2 9264 3278
networkweb@networkservicescompany.com.au
United Kingdom Distributed by Australian Consolidated Press (UK),
phone (01604) 497 531 fax (01604) 497 533
books@acpuk.com
Canada Distributed by Whitecap Books Ltd,
phone (604) 980 9852 fax (604) 980 8197
customerservice@whitecap.ca www.whitecap.ca
New Zealand Distributed by Netlink Distribution Company, phone (9) 366 9966
ask@ndc.co.nz
South Africa Distributed by PSD Promotions,
phone (27 11) 392 6065/6/7 fax (27 11) 392 6079/80
orders@psdprom.co.za

Clark, Pamela.
The Australian Women's Weekly
Fast pasta.
Includes index.
ISBN 978-1-96396-594-1
1. Cookery (Pasta).
I. Title. II Title: Australian women's weekly.
641.822
© ACP Magazines Ltd 2007
ABN 18 053 273 546

Cover Tagliatelle, chicken and peas in mustard cream sauce, page 307
Photographer Joshua Dasey
Stylist Justine Osborne
Food preparation Rebecca Squadrito
Additional photography Chris Chen
Photography page 10 Phillip Castleton, stylist Caryl Wiggins
Acknowledgments Lo Studio restaurant & bar, Annamaria Eoclidi of Pasta Emilia